Scottish Ceilidh Dancing

DAVID AND MAY EWART

MAINSTREAM
PUBLISHING

EDINBURGH AND LONDON

The authors are grateful to Mainstream Publishing for their faith in Scottish Ceilidh Dancing.

Reprinted, 2007

First published in Great Britain in 1996 by
MAINSTREAM PUBLISHING COMPANY (EDINBURGH) LTD
7 Albany Street
Edinburgh EH1 3UG

ISBN 9781851588459

A catalogue record for this book is available from
the British Library

Printed and bound in Great Britain by
Cox & Wyman Ltd

Contents

Introduction   7

Basic Holds, Steps and Figures
     Holds   11
     Steps and Figures   14
     Line of Dance   21

Simple as Shortcake
     Ceilidh Dances for Beginners   23

Kilted Capers
     Ceilidh Dances for Those that Ken a Wee Bit   73

Tartan Wizardry
     Challenging Ceilidh Dances   123

The Authors

David and May Ewart have spent a lifetime in dance. They are professional dance teachers with the United Kingdom Alliance of Professional Teachers of Dance and are actively involved in the teaching of ceilidh dancing. David and May are the resident dance instructors for Ceilidh and Sequence Dance holidays at Dunblane Hydro where they have worked with Jim McLeod and his Band for many years, and have also instructed Ceilidh dancing on P&O Canberra cruises.

David and May were previous winners of the British Inventive Dance competition when competing in Sequence Inventive Dance.

Introduction

The popularity of ceilidh dancing in Scotland has reached the stage where it can no longer be ignored as a serious rival to other types of dancing. Nowadays, even the small villages hold ceilidhs which continue to play a valuable role in social and community life. It is abundantly clear that this style of dance has an enormous following from all age groups. Young people discover that in ceilidh there is life after disco, and 'mature movers' are attracted by the nice-and-easy appeal of this form of dance, as well as by its social aspects. Those who turn to ceilidh from other styles of dance should recognise that here is a style which is easy to learn and can be danced enjoyably with the absolute minimum of tuition.

The task and purpose of *Scottish Ceilidh Dancing* is to open a door leading to a pleasurable recreation which will last a lifetime. We will transform the 'sitting-down dancers' into active dancers and will try to encourage you to attempt a form of dancing which has its roots in Scotland. Those who are more experienced can turn to the more complicated routines which, again, are described in plain, easy-to-understand language.

There are numerous dances in existence, but many of them fall into well-defined groups — learn one and you are well on your way to mastering the remainder of the group. One advantage of ceilidh is that most of the dance routines are repeated after a 16 or 32 bar sequence and, with the exception of set dances, all dancers will be performing the same routine at the same time.

Part of this book contains request dances, which have been included in response to a strong demand for them. It is also worth bearing in mind that many dancers live in out-of-the-way spots in Scotland and depend on others passing on dances. This can lead to a variation in dances in some districts and it is therefore easier for the novice to 'go with the flow'.

What is a ceilidh?

A ceilidh usually includes a piper, singers, highland dancers, poetry or indeed anyone or anything which makes up a Scottish social evening, and is normally followed by a dance.

What is a ceilidh dance?

A dance which includes popular Scottish traditional dances and some old-time dances; a modern waltz or a quickstep can even find their way into the programme.

When is the best time to begin ceilidh dancing?

Now! Ceilidh dancing attracts both the young and old, regardless of dancing skill. After mastering even a few of the dances in this book, you will find it quite easy to join in at any ceilidh gathering.

Dancing, and in particular Scottish dancing, is part of our

heritage; with your help we will keep ceilidh alive now and into the coming centuries.

Happy dancing!

Holds

Ballroom Hold

Dancers face their partners. The gentleman raises his left hand approximately to shoulder height and clasps the lady's right hand.

He then places his right hand under her left shoulder blade allowing her to rest her left hand on his upper right arm.

Open Hold

The lady stands on the gentleman's right side with her left hand in his right hand. Both partners face down the line of dance.

Double Hold

The partners stand facing each other. The lady's left hand is in the gentleman's right hand and her right hand in his left. Their joined arms are raised to the side and extended.

Shadow Hold

The partners face down the line of dance with the gentleman standing slightly behind the lady and to her left. His left hand holds her left hand at shoulder level, and his right hand holds her right hand over her right shoulder.

Side-by-Side Position

Both partners face down the line of dance with the lady on the gentleman's right. He places his right arm around her waist. She puts her left hand on his right shoulder.

Bower Hold

The lady turns under the gentleman's and lady's joined hands (left hand to left hand joined, right hand to right hand joined and the joined right hands are on top). As the lady turns to her right or left the joined hands are raised in a bower position to allow the lady to turn under.

Steps and Figures

Slip Step

This step is used in reels or jigs and in dancing circles. Step to the side on toes of left foot and close heel of right foot to heel of left foot. Step to the side on toes of right foot and close heel of left foot to heel of right foot. Continue in this manner.

Travelling Step

This step is used when covering a distance in dance, for example when dancing up or down a set. This simple step is used in ceilidh dancing, but not in Scottish Country Dancing.

Step forward on right foot (with weight) while weight is still on toe of left foot.
Bring left foot up behind right foot.
Take a small step forward with right foot and at the same time hop and bring left foot forward.
Step forward on left foot (with weight) while weight is still on toe of right foot.

Bring right foot up behind left foot.
Take a small step forward with left foot and at the same time hop and bring right foot forward.
Count for above 1-2-3, 1-2-3.

Pas de Basque

This step is a setting step.
Spring on to right foot.
Bring left foot in front of right foot almost closing to the instep of right foot.
Replace weight on to left foot.
Replace weight back on to right foot.
Repeat above with springing action on to left foot.
Pas de basque right and pas de basque left – count 1-2-3, 1-2-3.

Aerial

This is a position in which the foot is raised from the floor: low aerial is when the foot is level with the other ankle; medium aerial is level with calf; high aerial is level with knee.

Chassé

Step, close, step.

Pivot

A turn on one or both feet.

Forward Lock Step

Lock step to the left.
Place left foot forward.
Cross right foot behind left foot.
Left foot forward.

Lock step to the right.
Place right foot forward.
Cross left foot behind right foot.
Right foot forward.

Box or Square Step

Step to the side with left foot.
Close right foot to left foot.
Step back with left foot.
Step to side with right foot.
Close left foot to right foot.
Step forward with right foot

Balance

A transfer of weight forward and back.

Check

A checking action, usually outside partner.

Twinkle

Step close, step back.

Line of Dance
Following an anti-clockwise direction parallel to walls round the room.

Promenade Position
Gent's right hip to lady's left hip, both facing line of dance.

Counter Promenade Position
Gent's left hip in contact with lady's right hip, both facing against line of dance.

Advance and Retire
Three steps forward and close.
Three steps back and close.

Do-si-do
Facing partner, walk forward with partners passing right shoulder to right shoulder.
Step to the right behind partner.
Walk backwards, with partners passing left shoulder to left shoulder, to return to original position.

Cast off
Partners stand side-by-side, the lady on the gent's right. The lady turns to her right and dances down the line of dance on the outside of the set on her side.

Gent turns to his left and dances down the outside of set on his side

Right-Hand Star
Couples join their right hands above shoulder level and skip round to the right.

Left-Hand Star
Couples join their left hands above shoulder level and skip round to the left.

Ladies Chain
Two ladies give their right hand and change places.
They then give their left hand and turn each other's partner.
The ladies cross back, giving their right hands, and turn their own partner with the left hand until everyone is back in their original places.

Reel of Three or Figure of Eight
Should be self-explanatory by its title.
Three dancers interweave in a figure-of-eight formation.

Corners
The four corners in a set form a square.

The first couple dances into the centre, ending back-to-back diagonally across the set – the first gent faces the third lady and the first lady faces the second gent (first corners).

The first gent then turns to face the second lady and the first lady turns to face the third gent (second corners).

Rights and Lefts

This figure consists of two couples dancing in the formation of a square.

Commencing position – lady on gent's right side.

Ladies and gents dance across, giving right hands to their opposite partners and crossing over the set.

They face their own partners and give left hands to change places.

They face the partner opposite, give their right hands and change places.

They then face their own partners and give their left hands to change places and return to their original place.

Half rights and lefts is half of the above, finishing on opposite side.

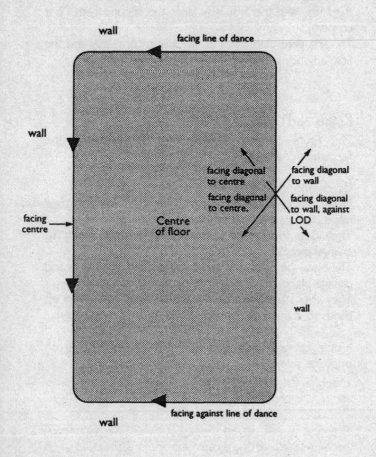

wall

facing line of dance

wall

wall

facing diagonal to centre

facing diagonal to wall

facing diagonal to centre.

facing diagonal to wall, against LOD

facing centre

Centre of floor

wall

wall

facing against line of dance

wall

LOD   line of dance

Line of Dance

Think of the line of dance as an imaginary line which travels round the ballroom, parallel to the walls. The dancers move in an anti-clockwise direction. So, when you 'move against the line of dance', you go along this line in a clockwise direction.

When you are instructed to 'stand facing the line of dance' the ballroom wall should be on your right and the centre of the floor on your left.

Diagonal to wall – facing midway between the line of dance and the wall

Diagonal to centre – facing midway between line of dance and centre

Diagonal to wall, against the line of dance – facing midway between the wall and against the line of dance

Diagonal to centre, against line of dance – facing midway between the centre and against line of dance
The diagram opposite may help.

Simple as Shortcake

Ceilidh Dances for Beginners

Barn Dance	25
Blue Danube Waltz	27
Boston Two-Step	29
Britannia Two-Step	31
Chicago Swing	33
Cuckoo Waltz	36
Dashing White Sergeant	38
Dinky One-Step	41
Eva Three-Step	43
Gay Gordons	45
Glyngarry Swing	47
Hesitation Waltz	50
Highland Schottische	52
Military Two-Step	55
Party Veleta	57
St Bernard's Waltz	59
Square Dance	61
Swedish Masquerade	64
Viennese Swing	67
White Heather Foxtrot	70

Barn Dance

An added bonus to learning this dance is that it will enable you to do two dances with similar steps, the English version and the Scottish Highland Barn dance.

Time 4/4
Tempo 32bpm

Commence this dance with both partners facing the line of dance in open hold – lady standing on the gent's right, her left hand holding his right hand.

The gent begins left foot forward down the line of dance (lady right foot).
Right foot forward down the line of dance.
Left foot forward down the line of dance.
Point right foot (lady points left foot).

Right foot back, against line of dance (lady left foot).
Left foot back, against line of dance.
Right foot back, against line of dance.
Point left foot (lady points right foot).
Bars 1–2

Move sideways away from your partner (gent to centre and lady wall) and release the hold.
Take three steps away from your partner (left, right, left).
Point right foot and clap.
Take three steps towards your partner (right, left, right).
Close to face your partner and take up ballroom hold.
   Bars 3–4

Step, close, step to gent's left.
Step, close, step to gent's right.
   Bars 5–6

Dance one and a half bars of natural waltz turn to the right (count 1-2-3, 2-2-3, 3-2-3) and open out, releasing the hold and moving back into starting position on 4-2-3.
   Bars 7–8

Highland Barn Dance

Time 2/4
Tempo 40bpm

Commence with the lady on the gent's right-hand side, his right arm should be round her waist and her left hand on his right shoulder.

Dance as above but instead of pointing the foot, hop. The natural turn at the end is danced, step, hop; step, hop on alternate feet to return to starting position.

Blue Danube Waltz

As the title suggests, the Blue Danube or a similar type of tune gives this dance a nice and easy relaxed rhythm. It is a perfect follow-up to a set dance.

Time: 3/4
Tempo: 46bpm

Commence in high shadow hold (as in Gay Gordons).

Lady chassés across in front of gent (step, close, step) moving to the left and centre.
Gent makes slight balancing action as he guides lady across.
Lady chassés across in front of gent (step, close, step), moving to the right and towards the wall.
Gent slight balancing action as he guides lady across to original position.
   Bars 1–4

Moving down line of dance.
Step, point; step, point.
Walk, one, two, three (left, right, left).
   Bars 5–8

Take three steps back, raising the right foot, then the left foot, and the right foot again.
Close the left foot to the right foot (lady closing without putting any weight on her left foot).
  Bars 9–12

Lady chassés across in front of gent, moving to the left and centre.
Gent makes slight balancing action as he guides lady across.
Lady chassés across in front of gent moving to the right and the wall.
Gent makes slight balancing action as he guides lady across to original position.
  Bars 13–16

Step, point; step, point.
Walk, one, two, three (left, right, left).
  Bars 17–20

Take two steps back, raising the right foot, then the left foot.
Close left foot to right foot without weight and turn to face the wall and your partner.
Take up ballroom hold.
  Bars 21–24

Chassé up line of dance (step, close, step).
Chassé against line of dance.
  Bars 25–28

Complete a natural waltz turn to the right (count 1-2-3, 2-2-3, 3-2-3) and on 4-2-3 release the hold and take up shadow hold, ready to begin again.
  Bars 29–32

Boston Two-Step

The figure which dominates this dance is the pas de basque. Study it well and practise it often as in Scottish ceilidh dancing you will get a lot of mileage out of this movement.

   Time: 6/8
   Tempo: 56bpm

Commence this dance in open hold with lady on gent's right-hand side, and lady's left hand in gent's right hand, both facing the line of dance.

Pas de basque to the left (lady to the right).
Pas de basque to the right (lady to the left).
Take three steps forward (left foot, right foot, left foot).
Pivot on step four (gent moves to the right, lady to the left) turning to face against the line of dance.
Having released the hold, lady now places her right hand in gent's left hand.
   Bars 1–4

Assume open position, facing against the line of dance.
Pas de basque to the right (lady to the left).
Pas de basque to the left (lady to the right).
Take three steps forward against the line of dance (right foot, left foot, right foot).
Pivot on step four (gent moves to the left, lady to the right) turning to end facing the wall and your partner.
Bars 5–8

While in this left-hand hold, adopt double hold.
Pas de basque to the left (lady to the right).
Pas de basque to the right (lady to the left).
Move your left foot to the side, along the line of dance.
Close your right foot to your left foot.
Move your left foot to the side, along the line of dance.
Close your right foot to your left foot.
Bars 9–12

Release the right-hand hold and adopt ballroom hold.
Dance a natural waltz turn to the right (1 a2, 2a2, 3a2) and open out to starting position on 4a2. Assume open hold, ready to begin again.
Bars 13–16

Britannia Two-Step

Danced in threes, this dance has the same formation as the Dashing White Sergeant and is just as popular. The formation is variable as a gentleman can dance with two ladies at the same time, or one lady with two gents. Indeed, you may adopt any arrangement you prefer. When danced progressively (changing partners), the Britannia Two-Step is a good mixer.

    We will describe this particular dance as being danced by one gent and two ladies.

Time: 6/8
Tempo: 56bpm

Begin in sets of three, all facing up the line of dance.
Gent stands in the centre with a lady on each side and joins hands with both ladies.
For bars 1–8 each person dances with the same foot:
All dance with left foot – heel, toe, slip step to the left, towards the centre.
All dance with right foot – heel, toe, slip step to the right, towards the wall.
    Bars 1–4

Take three steps forward, down the line of dance (left, right, left).
Kick your right foot forward.
Walk three steps backwards, against the line of dance (right, left, right).
Close your left foot to your right foot.
   Bars 5–8

All pas de basque left and then right with gent making a slight turn, first to the lady on his left and then to the lady on his right.
Gent pas de basque.
Then, as gent does his next pas de basque, he raises his arms and allows ladies to turn under his arms (the ladies should be turning to the left).
Alternatively, all three can release the hold and the ladies can make an outward turn to their right.
   Bars 9–12

Now you all should be back in your starting positions (in a set of three).
All take three steps forward, down the line of dance (left, right, left).
Kick right foot forward.
Take three steps backwards, against the line of dance (right, left, right).
Close your left foot to your right foot without weight and you are ready to recommence the dance.
   Bars 13–16

To make this dance progressive, the gent should move forward on the last three steps forward, allowing the ladies to go back to find a new partner behind.

Chicago Swing

This dance introduces us to another type of rhythm and adds a new challenge to both ceilidh bands and dancers.

    Time: 4/4
    Tempo: 48bpm

The dance commences with both dancers facing the line of dance, their inside arms should be joined.

Walk three steps forward (left, right, left) down the line of dance, lady walks right, left, right.
Close your right foot to your left foot.
Make a slight turn to your left (lady turns to her right) and point your left foot to the side (lady points her right foot).
Make a slight turn to face the line of dance again and close your left foot to your right foot without weight.
Make a slight turn to the left, point your left foot to the side and close your left foot to your right foot without weight.
    Bars 1–4

Move left foot forward down the line of dance.

Cross your right foot behind your left foot (this is called a lock step).

Move left foot forward down the line of dance.

Then move right foot forward down the line of dance.

Cross your left foot behind your right foot (and so you have performed a second lock step).

Move right foot forward down the line of dance.

Release the hold.

Make a solo outward turn (turn on three steps and close) to gent's left (lady's right) until you are facing the wall and your partner.

   Bars 5–8

Move your left foot forward towards the wall (lady moves right foot back).

Point your right foot forward (lady points her left foot back).

Move your right foot back towards the centre (lady moves her left foot forward).

Point your left foot back (lady points her right foot forward).

Move your left foot forward towards the wall (lady steps back with her right foot).

Point your right foot forward (lady points her left foot back).

Step back towards the centre with your right foot (lady places her left foot forward).

Point your left foot back (lady points her right foot forward).

   Bars 9–12, danced with Charleston action

With your left foot, step to the side, along the line of dance.

Close your right foot to your left.

Step to the side with your left foot, and this time sway

your body slightly to the left.

Now step to the side with your right foot, against the line of dance.

Close your left foot to your right foot.

Move your right foot to the side, this time sway your body slightly to the right.

Move your left foot to the side and towards the centre (lady moves her right foot towards the wall).

Drag your right foot to your left foot without weight and clap.

Move your right foot to the side, towards the wall and your partner.

Drag your left foot to your right foot without weight and link arms with your partner ready to recommence dance.

Bars 13–16

Cuckoo Waltz

Ceilidh bands can help to make this dance popular by their choice of tunes — fortunately, there is a tune of the same name and this would be our choice.

Time: 3/4
Tempo: 48bpm

Begin the Cuckoo Waltz in ballroom hold, with gent facing the line of dance.

Balance forward and close (step forward on your left foot and close your right to your left foot, without weight).
Balance back and close without weight (step back on your right foot and close your left to your right foot, without weight).

Make a reverse waltz turn (turning to gent's left) to finish facing the wall and your partner.
   Bars 1–4

Assume double hold — partners stand facing each other with joined arms extended.

Step on to your left foot and swing your right foot across in front of it.

Step on to your right foot and swing your left foot across. Release the hold and, commencing with the inside foot, dance a solo outward waltz turn (the gent to his right, the lady to her left), moving against the line of dance to finish facing the wall and your partner.

Bars 5–8

Assume double hold.

Step, close, step, close, down the line of dance.

Step, close, step, close, against the line of dance.

Bars 9–12

Assume ballroom hold.

Dance a natural waltz turn to the right to finish facing the line of dance and ready to recommence the dance.

Bars 13–16

Dashing White Sergeant

Undoubtedly the jewel in the ceilidh crown. Danced to lively Scottish reels, the Dashing White Sergeant is a must for anyone connected with ceilidh dancing.

   Time: 6/8
   Tempo: 60bpm

One gent stands in the middle, flanked by a lady at each side, with their inside hands linked. Two groups of three face each other and the various sets of six dancers form a complete circle around the room.

Each set of six joins hands to form a small circle.
Circle to the left (clockwise) to the count of eight.
   Bars 1–4

Circle to the right (anti-clockwise) to the count of eight.
All fall back into original lines.
   Bars 5–8

Gent turns to the lady on his right and pas de basque to the right (the lady to the left).

Pas de basque to the left (lady to the right).
Assume double hold (or simply link arms with the lady) and turn her to the right.
Release your hold and end up by facing the lady on your left.
Bars 9–12

Pas de basque to the right (lady to the left).
Pas de basque to the left (lady to the right).
Assume double hold (or link arms with the lady) and turn her to the right.
Release the hold.
Bars 13–16

Face the lady on your right as you both begin to dance a figure of eight, passing first the lady on your right, your left shoulder to her left shoulder, and then pass the lady on your left, your right shoulder to her right shoulder. Meanwhile, the ladies follow the gent's figure of eight pattern.
Alternatively, this routine can be danced by linking arms with your partners and turning.
Bars 17–24

At end of the figure eight, the set of six divides into two lines of three dancers. With their inside hands linked, the lines face each other so that half the dancers in the room are dancing in a clockwise direction and the other half anti-clockwise.
The lines advance towards each other for three steps and then retire away from each other by taking three steps back.
Bars 25–28

As the lines of three advance towards each other once more, those moving in anti-clockwise direction raise their joined hands and allow the line moving clockwise (having released hold) to pass through their raised arms to meet a new line of three.

Get ready to repeat the routine.

Bars 29–32

Dinky One-Step

This is a very easy dance to learn, and is especially useful as an introduction to ballroom hold. It can be danced to sing-along music, which makes the Dinky One-Step as much fun as its name suggests.

   Time: 6/8 or 2/4
   Tempo: 65bpm

Begin in ballroom hold with gent facing the line of dance.

Point your left foot forward, keeping your weight on the right foot (lady should point her right foot back).
Point your left foot back, keeping your weight on the right foot (lady should point her right foot forward).
Take four steps down the line of dance (left, right, left, right).
   Bars 1–4

Point your left foot forward, keeping your weight on the right foot (lady points her right foot back).
Point your left foot back, keeping your weight on the right foot (lady points her right foot forward).

Take four steps down the line of dance (left, right, left, right).

Bars 5—8

Point your left foot to the side quickly (lady points her right foot to the side).
Close your left foot to your right foot quickly.
Point your right foot to the side quickly.
Close your right foot to your left foot quickly.

Step to the side with your left foot.
Close right foot to left foot.
Step to the side with your right foot.
Close left foot to right foot.
(These last four steps can be danced as two pas de basque).

Bars 9—12

Take four steps forward (left, right, left, right).
Pivot to the right to end in starting position.

Bars 13—16

Alternatively, the four steps and pivot can be danced as two full natural turns in two-step timing.

Eva Three-Step

This is a dance that fills the floor at any ceilidh. It is largely made up of three steps plus a point and so it should not prove difficult even for the novice dancer.

Time: 4/4
Tempo: 32bpm

Begin this dance in open hold with lady's left hand in gent's right hand. Both should be facing the line of dance.

Take three steps forward down the line of dance, gent: left, right, left; and lady: right, left, right.
On the fourth step point your right foot forward and, making a slight turn, face your partner.
After releasing the hold, gent takes three steps to his right (right, left, right) passing behind lady as she takes three steps to her left (left, right, left) passing in front of gent.
Point your left foot to the side and, making a slight turn, face your partner. You may, if you wish, clap your hands when you point your foot.
Bars 1–4

Gent takes three steps to the left, passing in front of lady (left, right, left).
He points his right foot forward, she points her left.
Assume open hold (lady's left hand in gent's right hand).
Take three steps backwards against the line of dance.
Gent: right, left, right. Lady: left, right, left.
Point your left foot to the side, facing the line of dance.
  Bars 5–8

Release hold and dance a solo outward waltz turn, gent turning to his left and lady to her right (1a2, 2a2).
End up facing partner and take up double hold.

Pas de basque to gent's left (lady's right) and pas de basque to gent's right (lady's left).
  Bars 9–12

Change from double hold into ballroom hold.
Dance two complete natural waltz turns (1a2, 2a2, 3a2, 4a2) opening out at the end to finish in side-by-side position, facing up the line of dance in open hold.
  Bars 13–16

Gay Gordons

This is a very lively Scottish party dance which has been popular for many years and still continues to find a prominent place at most ceilidh dances. In recent years it has been slightly modified, making it more enjoyable for the ladies who now don't have to dance until they are dizzy doing turns!

Time: 6/8
Tempo: 56bpm.

Begin this dance in shadow hold with both lady and gent facing the line of dance. The gent stands slightly behind the lady. His left hand holds her left hand at shoulder height. He takes her right hand in his right hand over her right shoulder.
Both gent and lady dance the same steps (with the same foot) as follows:

Both walk forward for three steps (left, right, left).
Go right foot forward while making a half turn to the right to end facing against the line of dance. (The lady should now be on the gent's left side.)

Now facing against the line of dance, walk back for four steps (left, right, left, right).
 Bars 1–4

Walk forward for three steps, still against the line of dance (left, right, left).
Go forward on the right foot against the line of dance, making a half turn to the left to end facing the line of dance. Both walk back four steps (left, right, left, right).
 Bars 5–8

The gent's and lady's steps are now different:
Release the left-hand hold. Gent raises his right arm to allow lady to turn two complete natural turns to the right under his raised arm.
Gent walks forward for four steps (left foot, right foot, left foot, right foot) and ends by facing the wall and his partner. Taking up ballroom hold, step to the side with your left foot, down the line of dance.
Close the right foot to the left foot.
Step to the side with the left foot, down the line of dance.
Close the right foot to the left foot.
 Bars 9–12

Dance a natural waltz turn (turn to right), opening out to finish in original starting position – (1a2, 2a2, 3a2, 4a2).
 Bars 13–16

Alternative version on bars 9 and 10 is as follows:
Pas de basque away from partner (gent to the left, lady to the right).
Pas de basque towards partner.
Pas de basque away from partner.
Pas de basque towards partner and then take up ballroom hold.

Glyngarry Swing

A lively party two-step to test your co-ordination of hand and foot movements.

Time: 6/8
Tempo: 48bpm

Begin in shadow hold with lady's left hand in gent's left hand at shoulder height. The gent should have his right hand on her right shoulder.

Both lady and gent dance with same foot for the following steps.

Both dance heel, toe, heel, toe using the left foot.
Step your left foot diagonally forward.
Cross your right foot behind your left foot (this is called a lock step).

Step your left foot diagonally forward and make a slight swivel to the right.

Step your right foot diagonally forward, towards the wall.

Cross the left foot behind the right foot (again, making a lock step).

Step your right foot forward diagonally to the wall and make a slight swivel to the left and face the line of dance.

Bars 1–4

Step left foot forward down the line of dance.

Step right foot forward down the line of dance.

Step left foot forward down the line of dance.

Swing your right foot forward, raising it slightly off the floor.

Travel right foot back, against the line of dance.

Travel left foot back, against the line of dance.

Travel right foot back, against the line of dance.

Close your left foot to your right foot (gent closing without weight, lady with weight).

Bars 5–8

At this point the partners' steps separate.

Release the hold and step away from your partner.

With his left foot, the gent steps to the side (lady steps with her right foot).

Close the right foot to the left foot without weight and clap hands facing the centre (the lady should be facing the wall).

Turn right (lady left) to face your partner.

Step to the side with your right foot.

Close your left foot to your right foot to face the wall and your partner. Clap.

Slightly bend your knees while simultaneously slapping them (left hand slaps left knee and right hand slaps right knee).

The partners then lightly clap their left hands together.

The partners then lightly clap their right hands together.

Then the partners clap both their hands together at the same time (gent's left hand claps lady's right hand and gent's right hand claps lady's left hand).

Bars 9–12

Turn to the left and face the line of dance (the lady turns to her right).

Take three diagonal steps forward, moving to the centre (lady moves towards the wall).

Commencing on the left foot (lady on her right foot), swing your right foot forward (lady swings her left foot) and across left foot, raising it slightly off the floor.

Clap at the same time.

Take three steps back (gent begins on the right foot, lady on the left foot), towards the wall and your partner.

Close the left foot to the right foot without weight, now facing down the line of dance and adopt shadow hold ready to recommence the dance.

Bars 13–16

Hesitation Waltz

This dance has many versions, but we have found the following routine to be the most popular.

Time: 3/4
Tempo: 46bpm

Begin in ballroom hold, facing the line of dance.
Balance forward and back. (Step forward on your left foot and close your right to your left foot, without weight. Then step back on your right foot and close your left to your right foot, without weight.)
Balance forward and back.

Alternatively:
As you balance forward, make a quarter turn to the left.
As you balance back, make a quarter turn to the left.
As you balance forward, make a quarter turn to the left.
As you balance back, make a quarter turn to the left.
Finally make one complete turn to end facing the line of dance.
   Bars 1—4

Walk two steps down the line of dance (left, right).
Run three steps down the line of dance (left, right, left).
   Bars 5–8

Walk three steps backwards down the line of dance
(right, left, right).
Turn to face down the line of dance and curtsy on the
fourth step.
   Bars 9–12

Make a natural waltz turn to the right (count 1-2-3, 2-2-3, 3-2-3, 4-2-3) ready to recommence the dance.
   Bars 13–16

Highland Schottische

The name of this dance tends to draw most Scots to it and, as it is only an eight-bar sequence, it can be learned very quickly. Once mastered, its polka-type rhythm will bring a lift to any ceilidh.

   Time: 2/4
   Marching tune

Begin in ballroom hold with gent facing the wall and lady facing the centre.
Gent turns slightly to the left and lady to the right.

Standing on the ball of his right foot, gent points his left foot to the side (lady stands on left foot and points her right foot).
Quickly lift your left foot behind your right leg.
Gent points his left foot to the side (lady points her right foot).
Quickly lift your left foot in front of your right leg (lifting it to about calf-height).
(The above steps are danced with a hopping action on the right foot (lady hops on her left foot).)

Step to the side with the left foot (lady steps with her right foot).

Close your right foot to your left foot.

Step to side with the left foot and, while hopping on the ball of your left foot, bring the right foot behind the left leg (lady hops on her right foot, bringing the left one behind).

Turn slightly to gent's right (lady's left) to face against the line of dance.

Gent points his right foot to the side (lady points her left foot).

Quickly lift your right foot behind your left leg.

Gent points his right foot to the side (lady points her left foot).

Quickly lift your right foot in front of your left leg (lifting it to about calf-height).

(The above steps are danced with a hopping action on the left foot (lady hops on her right foot).)

Step to the side with your right foot.

Close your right foot to your left foot.

Step to the side with your right foot and, while hopping on the ball of your right foot, bring your left foot behind your right leg (lady hops on her left foot, bringing the right one behind).

Bars 1–4

Step to the side with your left foot.

Close your right foot to your left foot.

Step to the side with your left foot.

Bring your right foot behind your left leg while hopping on the ball of your left foot (lady's right).

Step to the side with your right foot.

Close your left foot to your right foot.

Step to the side with your right foot.
Bring your left foot behind your right leg while hopping on the ball of your right foot (lady's left).

Turn to the right.
Step and hop on alternate feet to complete the sequence.
   Bars 5–8

We are now ready to begin the dance again.

Military Two-Step

This party version of a championship old-time dance has many variations, especially on bars 1 and 2 and bars 5 and 6. Select the version you are happy with and enjoy this dance!

Time: 6/8 or 2/4
Tempo: 56bpm

Begin in side-by-side position with lady on gent's right. His right arm should be round lady's waist with her left hand resting on his right shoulder. Both should be facing the line of dance.
Gent taps his left heel forward, down the line of dance, without weight (lady taps her right heel).
Gent taps his left toe backwards (slightly to the side). Lady taps her right toe backwards).
Walk three steps down the line of dance (left, right, left). Release the hold and turn to the right on step four (lady turns to her left) to end facing against the line of dance.
Now gent's left arm should be around lady's waist and her right hand should be on his left shoulder.
Bars 1–4

Gent taps his right heel forward, against the line of dance, without weight (lady taps her left heel).

Gent taps his right toe backwards (slightly to the side). Lady's taps her left toe backwards.

Walk three steps against the line of dance (right, left, right).

Release the hold and turn to the left on step eight to end facing the wall and your partner.

   Bars 5–8

Take up double hold.

Jump on your left foot and kick your right foot across to the right side of your partner.

Jump on your right foot and kick your left foot across to the left side of your partner.

Gent takes two small steps to his left while lady completes an underarm turn to right under gent's raised left arm.

   Bars 9–12

Take up ballroom hold.

Waltz to the right (1a2, 2a2, 3a2) and on 4a2 return to starting position.

   Bars 13–16

Party Veleta

This party version of the Veleta is the one which is more commonly used in ceilidh.

Begin by taking up double hold, facing your partner and the wall (lady is facing the centre).

Step to the side with your left foot, along the line of dance.
Swing your right foot across your left foot, along the line of dance.
Step to the side with your right foot, against the line of dance.
Swing left foot across right foot, against the line of dance.
Step to side with left foot, along the line of dance.
Slowly close your right foot to your left foot.
Step to side with left foot, along the line of dance.
Slowly close your right foot to your left foot.
   Bars 1–4

Step to the side with your right foot, against the line of dance.
Swing your left foot across your right foot, against the line of dance.

Step to the side with your left foot, along the line of dance.

Swing your right foot across your left foot, along the line of dance.

Step to the side on your right foot, against the line of dance.

Slowly close your left foot to your right foot.

Step to the side on your right foot, against the line of dance.

Slowly close your left foot to your right foot.

Bars 5–8

Gent releases lady's left hand and places his right hand under her left shoulder to take up ballroom hold.

Make one complete natural waltz turn to the right to end facing the wall (count 1-2-3, 2-2-3).

Release the hold and resume double hold.

Travel left foot to side (lady's right foot) along the line of dance.

Slowly close your right foot to your left foot.

Travel left foot to side along the line of dance.

Slowly close your right foot to your left foot.

Bars 9–12

Release the double hold and again take up ballroom hold.

Dance four bars of natural waltz, turning to gent's right (count 1-2-3, 2-2-3, 3-2-3, 4-2-3).

Release the ballroom hold and take up double hold, ready to begin the dance again.

Bars 13–16

St Bernard's Waltz

The St Bernard's Waltz is very popular with all age groups. It is easy to learn and the foot stamping which comes at the beginning adds a bit of novelty to this particular dance.

Time: 3/4
Tempo: 48bpm

Begin in ballroom hold with gent facing the wall and lady facing the centre.

Step to the side with your left foot (lady steps with her right foot).
Close your right foot to your left foot.
Step to the side with your left foot.
Close your right foot to your left foot.
Step to the side with your left foot.
Close your right foot to your left foot with a little stamping action.
Replace the weight on to your left foot, again with a little stamping action.
Bars 1–4

Step to the right with your right foot (lady steps with her left foot), against the line of dance.

Close your left foot to your right foot.

Step to the side with your right foot, against the line of dance.

Close your left foot to your right foot without weight.

Move your left foot back towards the centre.

Move your right foot back towards the centre.

Bars 5–8

Step forward towards the wall with your left foot.

Step forward towards the wall with your right foot.

Gent releases his right-hand hold around lady's waist but keeps her right hand in his left.

Gent steps to side with his left foot and raises his left arm, allowing lady to turn to her right under his raised arm.

His right foot closes to his left foot while she completes her turn to the right under the raised arms.

Bars 9–12

Take up ballroom hold.

Make a natural waltz turn (to the right) for four bars, ending when gent faces the wall and lady faces the centre, ready to start again.

Bars 13–16

Square Dance

With its easy movements and minimum of turns, the Square Dance provides an ideal introduction to set dancing. Don't be surprised to find this dance called another name at some ceilidhs as each district in Scotland tends to adopt their own name for it.

Time: 6/8
Tempo: 48bpm

This set dance is for four couples. The ladies stand facing the gents, with the top couple nearest the stage (and the band). The gent's left shoulder should be next to the stage and he should be standing opposite his partner.
All advance towards each other for two steps.
All clap your right hand against that of the person opposite you three times.
All take two steps back and stamp three times.
   Bars 1–4

All advance two steps towards each other.
All clap your left hand against that of the person opposite you three times.

All take two steps back and stamp three times.
  Bars 5–8

Now perform a do-si-do – skip towards your partner opposite and pass right shoulder to right shoulder. Step to your right – you should be back to back – and then pass left shoulder to left shoulder and return to your original place.
  Bars 9–12

Next is a see-saw (basically, this is the reverse of the sequence above). Skip towards your partner opposite and pass left shoulder to left shoulder. Step to your left – you should be back to back – and then pass right shoulder to right shoulder and return to your original place.
  Bars 13–16

The first couple now join hands and skip sideways down between the lines for a count of eight. Meanwhile, the other couples clap their hands in time to the music.
  Bars 17–20

The first couple now skip sideways back up between the lines for a count of eight (the other couples continue to clap).
  Bars 21–24

The first couple now cast off – gent turns to his left and dances down the outside of the set. All other gents turn left and follow him. The ladies turn right, following the first lady down the outside of the set.
  Bars 25–28

The first couple now form an arch at the opposite end of

the set. With both hands joined and held high, they allow the other couples to pass underneath.

Once all the dancers have passed through, the first couple release each other's hands and keep their position at the end of the set. Now the second couple are at the top of the set and are ready to repeat the dance.

Bars 29–32

Swedish Masquerade

This is a dance which combines three different tempos but it is easy once you have mastered the pas de basque. The slow rhythm in bars 1–16 give you time to get your breath back after your pas de basque in reel time.

Slow March – 16 bars
Waltz – 16 bars
Reel – 16 bars

Begin in open hold, lady on gent's right side with her left hand in his right hand. Both should be facing the line of dance.
Slowly march forward for seven steps (gent commencing on his left foot and lady on her right).
Release the hold and turn to the right (lady turns left) on step eight to face against the line of dance. Now the gent takes the lady's right hand in his left.
Slowly march forward for seven steps, against the line of dance.
Release the hold and turn to the left (lady turns right) on step eight to face the line of dance.
   Slow march, bars 1–8

Gent takes lady's left hand in his right hand.

Pas de basque away from your partner (gent stepping to his left and lady to her right).

Pas de basque towards partner.

Pas de basque away from partner.

Pas de basque towards your partner and release hold.

Now take up ballroom hold.

Waltz to the gent's right for two complete turns (1a2, 2a2, 3a2, 4a2).

   Bars 9–16

Release the hold and take up open hold in side-by-side position with lady's left hand in gent's right hand.

Pas de basque away from your partner (gent stepping to his left and lady to her right).

Pas de basque towards your partner.

Pas de basque away from your partner.

Pas de basque towards your partner and release hold.

Now take up ballroom hold.

Waltz to the gent's right for two complete turns.

   Waltz, bars 1–8

Release the hold and take up an open hold in side-by-side position with lady's left hand in gent's right hand.

Pas de basque away from your partner (gent stepping to his left and lady to her right).

Pas de basque towards your partner.

Pas de basque away from your partner.

Pas de basque towards your partner and take up ballroom hold.

Waltz to the gent's right for two complete turns.

   Bars 9–16

Release the hold and take up open hold in side-by-side position (lady's left hand in gent's right hand).

Pas de basque away from your partner.

Pas de basque towards your partner.

Pas de basque away from your partner.

Pas de basque towards your partner then take up ballroom hold.

Waltz to the gent's right for two complete turns in reel tempo.

Reel, bars 1–8

Release hold and take up open hold in side by side position (lady's left hand in gent's right hand).

Pas de basque away from your partner.

Pas de basque towards your partner.

Pas de basque away from your partner.

Pas de basque towards your partner and take up ballroom hold.

Waltz to the gent's right for two complete turns in reel tempo.

Release the hold, take up open hold and assume starting position.

Bars 9–16

Viennese Swing

Danced to beautiful Viennese music, this dance can become the musical highlight of the evening.

   Time: 3/4
   Tempo: 48bpm

Begin in double hold with gent facing the wall and his partner.

Step left foot to side, along the line of dance (lady steps with her right).
Swing your right foot across your left foot.
Step right foot to side, against the line of dance.
Swing your left foot across your right foot.
Chassé to the left (step, close, step).
   Bars 1–4

Step right foot to side, against the line of dance (lady steps with her left).
Swing your left foot across your right foot.
Step left foot to side, along the line of dance.
Swing your right foot across your left foot.

Chassé to right (step, close, step).
   Bars 5–8

Balance towards your partner (step forward on your left foot, close your right foot to your left foot without weight).
Balance away from your partner (step back your right foot, close your left foot to your right foot without weight).
Gent releases lady's left hand.
Waltz to each other's places, passing left hip to left hip and lady turning under gent's left arm. Now gent should be facing the centre (lady facing the wall).
   Bars 9–12

Balance towards your partner.
Balance away from your partner.
Gent releases lady's left hand.
Waltz back to your own place, passing left hip to left hip and lady turning under gent's left arm. Now gent is again facing the wall and his partner.
Take up double hold.
   Bars 13–16

Step left foot forward, along the line of dance.
Step right foot forward, along the line of dance.
Chassé (step, close, step) along the line of dance and turn on the last step to face against the line of dance.
   Bars 17–20

Step right foot forward, against the line of dance.
Step left foot forward, against the line of dance.
Chassé (step, close, step) against the line of dance.
   Bars 21–24

Take two steps back to the centre (left, right). Lady steps forward (right, left).
Take two steps forward to the wall (left, right). Lady steps back (right, left).
   Bars 25–28

Take up ballroom hold.
Waltz to the right (1a2, 2a2, 3a2, 4a2), turning to end facing the wall and your partner in double hold.
   Bars 29–32

White Heather Foxtrot

This very simple dance with its Scottish name has only recently been added to ceilidh, but it has proved to be very popular with all dancers.

Time: 4/4
Tempo: 30bpm

Begin in ballroom hold with gent facing up the line of dance.

Walk two steps forward (left, right). (Slow, slow.)
Run three steps forward (left, right, left). (Quick, quick, slow.)
Walk two steps back against the line of dance (right, left). (Slow, slow.)
Run three steps back against the line of dance (right, left, right). (Quick, quick, slow.)
Bars 1–4

Lady turns slightly to her right, so that her left hip is against gent's right hip and both are facing the centre (this is the promenade position).

Take two steps forward towards the centre (left, right). (Slow, slow.)
Move your left foot forward towards the centre.
Close your right foot to your left foot.
Move your left foot forward towards the centre and swivel to gent's right (lady's left) to finish facing the wall. (Quick, quick, slow.)

Having turned to face the wall (now gent's left hip is against lady's right hip) and both are facing the wall.
Take two steps towards the wall (right, left). (Slow, slow.)
Right foot forward towards the wall.
Close your left foot to your right foot.
Move your right foot to the side.
Still in ballroom hold, lady makes a slight turn to her left, now you are facing up the line of dance. (Quick, quick, slow.)
   Bars 5–8

Walk three steps forward (left, right, left).
Balance back on to your right foot with a rocking action. (Slow, slow, slow, slow.)
Walk three steps forward (left, right, left).
Balance back on to your right foot, again with a rocking action. (Slow, slow, slow, slow.)
   Bars 9–12

Next, you are going to perform a double square.
Step left foot forward down the line of dance.
Move your right foot to the side.
Close your left foot to your right foot. (Slow, quick, quick.)
Step right foot back against the line of dance.
Move your left foot to the side.
Close your right foot to your left foot to complete the square. (Slow, quick, quick.)

Step left foot forward down the line of dance.
Move your right foot to the side.
Close your left foot to your right foot. (Slow, quick, quick.)
Step right foot back against the line of dance.
Move your left foot to the side.
Close your right foot to your left foot to complete the second square. (Slow, quick, quick.)
  Bars 13–16

Kilted Capers

Ceilidh Dances for Those that Ken a Wee Bit

Blues Glide	75
Circassian Circle	77
Flirtation Two-Step	79
Four-Hand Star	82
Friendly Waltz	85
Gay Gordons Two-Step	87
Gypsy Tap	90
Lomond Waltz	92
Lucky Seven	95
Marine Four-Step	97
Mississippi Dip	100
Pride of Erin Waltz	103
Southern Rose Waltz	106
Square Tango	109
Strip the Willow	112
Veleta	114
Victory Waltz	117
Waltz of the Bells	120

Blues Glide

The Blues Glide is a new dance to ceilidh. As its name denotes, a special feature of the dance is the glide step.

Time: 4/4
Tempo: 30bpm

Begin this dance in ballroom hold with gent facing up the line of dance.

Walk two steps forward (left, right).
Run three steps forward (left, right, left).
Walk two steps forward (right, left).
Run three steps forward (right, left, right).
   Bars 1—4

Now for the glide step.
Stamp your left foot.
Point your right foot to the side.
Bring your right foot behind your left foot.
Move your left foot to the side.
Step your right foot to side.
Drag your left foot to your right foot.

Repeat the glide.
  Bars 5–8

Run three steps back down the line of dance (left, right, left) and point your right foot back.
Run three steps forward down the line of dance (right, left, right) and point your left foot forward.
Full chassé turn to the right (step, close, step, and step, close, step). Repeat and finish facing the line of dance.
  Bars 9–12

Step left foot forward and point your right foot.
Right foot forward and point left foot.

Now for another glide.
Stamp your left foot.
Point your right foot to the side.
Bring your right foot behind your left foot.
Move your left foot to the side.
Step your right foot to side.
Without putting weight on your left foot drag it to your right foot. Now you are ready to start again.
  Bars 13–16

Circassian Circle

There are many versions of this dance. We've chosen the version which is danced in our area, but whichever adaptation you use we are sure you will enjoy the Circassian Circle.

32-bar jig or the original tune for the Circassian Circle
All the dancers form a circle with their hands joined. Lady stands on gent's right-hand side.

All advance four steps towards the centre.
All retire four steps back towards the wall.
   Bars 1–4

All advance four steps towards the centre.
All retire four steps back towards the wall.
   Bars 5–8

Release the hold.
Ladies advance four steps towards the centre and clap your hands.
Ladies retire four steps back towards the wall.
   Bars 9–12

Gents advance four steps towards the centre and clap your hands.
Gent turns to his right and walks four steps forward to meet his partner.*
    Bars 13–16

Gent swings his partner with propelled pivot steps to his right. (You can do this either by crossing your hands or by putting your right hand around each other's waist.) Swing for a count of 16.
    Bars 17–24

Release hold and take up shadow hold.
Both turn to the right.
Each couple now promenades anti-clockwise around the room for a count of 16 (skip, lock, step). On the last count both turn to face the centre.
Everyone join hands in a circle ready to recommence.
    Bars 25–32

*If the gent turns to the lady on his left and swings her, the dance is then a progressive dance.

Flirtation Two-Step

The Flirtation Two-Step introduces the zig-zag instead of repeated, dizzy-making turns. Once this step has been mastered, it can be used in many other dances.

Time: 6/8
Tempo: 48bpm

Begin in double hold with gent facing the wall and lady facing the centre.

Step right foot forward, across your left foot, along the line of dance.
Gent steps to the side with his left foot.
Put your right foot behind your left foot.
Gent steps to the side with his left foot, and so completes the zig-zag.
Put your right foot forward, across left foot, releasing the left-hand hold (this step is called a check).
Replace weight on to your left foot and take up double hold.
Chassé to right, against the line of dance (step, close, step).
Bars 1–4

Put your left foot forward, across your right foot, moving against the line of dance.

Gent steps to the side with his right foot.

Place your left foot behind your right foot.

Gent steps to the side with his right foot and completes a second zig-zag.

Put your left foot forward, across your right foot, in a check step and release the right-hand hold.

Replace weight on to your right foot and take up double hold.

Chassé to the left, along the line of dance (step, close, step).

   Bars 5–8

Release hold. Gent takes lady's left hand in his right (as in the open position), facing the line of dance.

Now you both perform three skipping lock steps down the line of dance as below:

Step right foot forward along the line of dance (lady steps with her left foot).

Cross your left foot behind your right foot (lady crosses right behind left). This is called a lock step.

Step right foot forward along the line of dance (lady steps with her left foot).

Step left foot forward down the line of dance (lady steps with her right foot).

Cross your right foot behind your left foot (lady crosses left behind right) in a lock step.

Step left foot forward down the line of dance (lady steps with her right foot).

Step right foot forward down the line of dance (lady steps with her left foot).

Cross your left foot behind your right foot (lady crosses right behind left) in a lock step.

Step right foot forward down the line of dance (lady steps with her left foot).

Close your right foot to your left foot, still facing the line of dance.

   Bars 9–12

Release the hold. Gent moves to face the centre, lady faces the wall.

Move your left foot to the side (lady steps to her right).

Place your right foot across your left foot.

Move your left foot to the side and swing your right foot across and clap your hands.

Move back to face the wall and your partner (lady faces the centre).

Move your right foot to the side.

Place your left foot across your right foot.

Move your right foot to the side and close your left foot to your right foot while moving slightly to the right to face your partner and the wall.

Take up double hold ready to recommence dance.

   Bars 13–16

Four-Hand Star

Undoubtedly one of the most popular ceilidh dances. As well as being a good introduction to set dancing, the Four-Hand Star is easy to dance and is an excellent mixer.

Time 4/4
Any good jig tune

Form a set of four made up of two couples – one couple faces the line of dance and the other faces against the line of dance. Lady stands on gent's right side.

All join your right hands together. Raise them slightly towards the centre in a star formation.
All dance four skipping steps round to the right for a count of four (this is called a right-hand wheel).
Bars 1–4

Release the hold and join your left hands, again slightly raised towards the centre in a star formation.
All dance four skipping steps round to the left for a count of four (this is called a left-hand wheel).
Bars 5–8

This is followed by a routine called a Ladies Chain:
Ladies join their right hands together and turn each other while gents move into ladies' places.
Then lady turns the gent opposite her by taking his left hand in her left hand.
Ladies join their right hands together and turn each other until facing partner.
Lady turns her partner by taking his left hand in her left hand until she arrives back in her original position.

    Bars 9–16

Dance towards the person opposite and pass right shoulder to right shoulder. Step to your right – you should now be back to back – and then pass left shoulder to left shoulder and return to your original place. Turn to face your own partners on the last step. (This routine is called a do-si-do.)

    Bars 17–20

Now repeat the do-si-do with your own partner: dance towards your partner, pass right shoulder to right shoulder, step to your right (you and your partner are back to back) and then pass left shoulder to left shoulder to return to your original place.
Turn to face the couple opposite.

    Bars 21–24

Join hands with your partner and advance to meet the other couple.
Step back from other couple.

    Bars 25–28

Advance once more towards other couple. The couple who are moving against the line of dance raise their joined arms to allow the other couple (who can now release their hold) to pass under and meet a new couple.

Bars 29–32

Friendly Waltz

As its name suggests, this is a friendly 'get together' dance which can be used at the beginning of a ceilidh to introduce dancers to new partners.

Time: 3/4
Tempo: 48bpm

All the dancers form a circle round the room, lady on gent's left, and all join hands.

All step forward on your left foot and swing your right foot towards the centre, raising it slightly off the floor.
All step back and close feet together.
Gent releases the hand of the lady on his right. Then, still holding the hand of the lady on his left he leads her round to his right-hand side.
All join hands again
Bars 1–4

All step forward on your left foot and swing your right foot towards the centre, raising it slightly off the floor.
All step back and close feet together.

Gent releases the hand of the lady on his left.
Lady holding gent's hand takes him as her partner and faces him and the wall. Gent bows slightly and lady curtsies.
   Bars 5–8

Take up ballroom hold with your new partner.
Dance: step, close, step to the gent's left.
Dance: step, close, step to the gent's right.
   Bars 9–12

Dance four bars of natural waltz (1a2, 2a2, 3a2, 4a2), turning to the right.
Open out on fourth bar to end with gent in the middle, with his own partner on his right and the new partner on his left.
Reform the circle, all join hands and prepare to repeat the dance.
   Bars 13–16

Gay Gordons Two-Step

The Gay Gordons Two-Step is a good introductory dance which is fun and easy to dance. Like the Britannia Two-Step, this dance is a good mixer when danced progressively (changing partners).

Time: 6/8
Tempo: 56bpm

Begin in open hold, facing down the line of dance. The lady should be on gent's right side, her left hand in his right.

Step left foot forward, along the line of dance (lady steps with her right foot).
Step right foot forward, along the line of dance (lady, left foot).
Step left foot forward, along the line of dance (lady, right foot).
Point right foot forward (lady points her left foot).

Gent crosses behind lady, keeping hold of her left hand. Lady turns to her left and passes under their joined, raised

arms to end both facing against the line of dance.
Step right foot forward, moving towards the wall and
raising your joined hands.
Step left foot forward towards the wall. Gent passes
behind lady and she does her underarm turn.
Step right foot forward, moving towards the wall.
Point left foot forward, against the line of dance.
Now you both should be facing against the line of dance
in an open side-by-side position.
   Bars 1–4

Step left foot forward, against the line of dance (lady's left
hand should still be in gent's right hand).
Step right foot forward, against the line of dance.
Step left foot forward, against the line of dance.
Point your right foot forward, against the line of dance.

Gent crosses behind lady, keeping hold of her left hand.
Lady passes in front of gent to his other side and ends
facing the line of dance.
Step right foot forward, moving towards the centre and
raising your joined hands.
Step left foot forward towards the centre. Gent passes
behind lady and she does her underarm turn.
Step right foot forward, moving towards the centre.
Point your left foot forward, up the line of dance.
Now you both should be facing the line of dance in open
hold.
   Bars 5–8

Release the hold.
Gent makes a quarter turn to his left and lady turns to her
right (in two-step timing).
Continue turning another quarter to the left (lady to the

right) to end facing the wall and your partner.
Gent pas de basque to his left (lady to her right) and pas
de basque to right (lady left).
  Bars 9–12

Moving away from your partner, gent steps his left foot
back towards the centre (lady steps her right foot back
towards the wall).
Step right foot back towards the centre (lady steps left
foot towards the wall).
Step left foot back towards the centre (lady steps right
foot towards the wall).
Raise your right foot off the floor to about calf-height.

Still facing your partner, move towards him/her.
Step right foot forward towards the wall (lady left foot to
the centre).
Left foot forward to the wall (lady right foot to the
centre).
Step right foot forward towards the wall (lady left foot to
the centre).
Point left your foot to the side and turn to face the line of
dance in an open side-by-side position.
  Bars 13–16

To make this dance progressive, gent moves forward on
the last three steps to find a new partner.

Gypsy Tap

This dance is very popular and is worthy of inclusion in any ceilidh programme as it is easy to learn.

Time: 6/8
Tempo: 56bpm

Begin by taking up ballroom hold with gent facing the wall and lady facing the centre.
Side close, side close, step left, right, left and close right foot to left foot along the line of dance.
Bars 1–4

Repeat the above.
Bars 5–8

Lady turns slightly to left to face against the line of dance.
Side close, side close, step right, left, right and close left foot to right foot against line of dance.
Bars 9–12

Repeat the above
Bars 13–16

Release hold and take up open hold with gent's right hand in lady's left hand.

Pas de basque to gent's left (lady's right).

Pas de basque to gent's right (lady's left).

Make an outward solo turn to gent's left (lady's right). 1a2, 2a2

Bars 17–20

Pas de basque to gent's left (lady's right).

Pas de basque to gent's right (lady's left).

Make an outward solo turn to gent's left (lady's right). 1a2, 2a2

Bars 21–24

Change to double hold.

Take three steps (left, right, left) back towards the centre (lady moves forward towards the centre) and tap your right foot (lady taps her left foot).

Take three steps forward towards the wall (right, left, right) and close feet.

Bars 25–28

Take up ballroom hold.

Chassé turn to right (1a2, 2a2, 3a2, 4a2) and end up facing the wall, ready to recommence.

Bars 29–32

Lomond Waltz

This is a firm favourite at all ceilidhs – perhaps its popularity has something to do with its Scottish name.

Time: 3/4
Tempo: 46bpm

Begin the waltz in ballroom hold with gent facing the wall and lady facing the centre.

Gent steps left foot to side, along the line of dance (lady steps with her right foot).
Close your right foot to your left foot.
Gent steps left foot to side, along the line of dance.
Close your right foot to your left foot without weight (this is known as a brush step).
Step right foot back towards the centre.
Step left foot back towards the centre.
   Bars 1–4

Step right foot to side, against the line of dance.
Close your left foot to your right foot.
Step right foot to side, against the line of dance.

Close your left foot to your right foot without weight (again performing a brush step).
Step left foot forward towards the wall.
Step right foot forward towards the wall and complete the square.

Bars 5–8

Release the hold. Gent takes lady's left hand in his right.
In the following steps, gent turns to his left and lady turns to her right.
Step left foot forward down the line of dance and start to make your turn.
Step right foot to side, facing the centre.
Close your left foot to your right foot and now you should be back to back with your partner.
Step left foot forward against the line of dance, continuing to turn.
Step right foot to side, facing the wall.
Close your left foot to your right foot and now you should be facing the wall and your partner.
Take up double hold.

Bars 9–12

Balance to your partner (step forward on your left foot and close your right foot to your left without weight).
Balance away from your partner (step back on your right foot and close your left foot to your right foot).
Gent releases lady's left hand and you waltz to each other's places, passing left hip to left hip, lady turning under gent's left arm.
Gent should now be facing the centre, and lady facing the wall.

Bars 13–16

Take up double hold.

Balance to your partner.
Balance away from your partner.
Gent releases lady's left hand and you waltz back to your own place, again passing left hip to left hip with lady turning under gent's left arm.
End by facing the wall and your partner.
    Bars 17–20

Take up double hold.
Gent steps left foot to side, along the line of dance (lady steps with her right foot).
Cross your right foot over your left foot.
Point your left foot forward without weight.
Swivel to the right and close your left foot to your right foot.
    Bars 21–24

Gent steps right foot to side, against the line of dance (lady steps with her left foot).
Cross your left foot over your right foot.
Point your right foot forward without weight against the line of dance.
Swivel to the left and close your right foot to your left foot.
    Bars 25–28

Take up ballroom hold.
Make two complete natural waltz turns to the right (count 1-2-3, 2-2-3, 3-2-3, 4-2-3) and end up in starting position.
    Bars 29–32

Lucky Seven

New to ceilidh, the Lucky Seven dance is similar to the Circassian Circle. It is very simple to perform, in fact, if you can count to seven you can master this dance!

32-bar jig or Circassian Circle type music.

All the dancers form a circle with their hands joined. Lady stands on gent's right-hand side.

All advance four steps towards the centre.
All retire four steps back towards the wall.
   Bars 1–4

Ladies advance four steps towards the centre and clap your hands twice.
Ladies retire four steps back towards the wall.
   Bars 5–8

Gents advance four steps towards the centre and clap your hands twice.
Turn on fourth step to face the wall.
Move three steps forward to meet your partner and

close, facing partner on step four to take up double hold.
  Bars 9–12

Both side close to the centre (step, close, step).
Both side close to the wall.
  Bars 13–16

Gent takes partner's right hand in his right hand (this is called handshake hold) and you dance a chain, the gent moving anti-clockwise and lady moving clockwise. Take the right hand of your own partner for one count. Now, with your left hand, take the left hand of the next lady and count two (your partner will take the hand of the next gent). Continue alternating partners until you reach your seventh partner on the count of seven. Normally, everyone counts the seven counts out loud.
  Bars 17–24

Retain your handshake hold with the seventh partner.
Dance a pas de basque left and right.
Make a propelled pivot to turn right and end up back in the circle formation and ready to start the dance again.
  Bars 25–32

Marine Four-Step

This lively dance is simple to learn and you'll find it is welcomed by all levels of ceilidh dancers.

Time: 6/8
Tempo: 56bpm

Begin this dance in open hold, facing the line of dance. Lady stands on gent's right side, her left hand in his right.

Step left foot forward, down the line of dance (lady steps with her right foot).
Step right foot forward, down the line of dance (lady steps with her left foot).
Step left foot forward, down the line of dance (lady steps with her right foot).
Hop on your left foot and at the same time point your right foot forward, raising it slightly off the floor (lady hops on right foot and points left foot).
Step right foot back, against the line of dance (lady, left foot).
Step left foot back, against the line of dance (lady, right foot).

Step right foot back, against the line of dance (lady, left foot).

Hop on your right foot and at the same time point your left foot forward, raising it slightly off the floor (lady hops on left foot and points right foot).

Bars 1–4

Still in open hold pas de basque to gent's left (lady's right).

Pas de basque to gent's right.

Release the hold.

Dance a solo waltz turn, gent turning to his left and lady to her right (1a2, 2a2).

End by facing the wall and your partner and take up double hold.

Bars 5–8

Step left foot to side, along the line of dance (moving to the left, lady to the right).

Cross your right foot over your left foot, along the line of dance.

Step left foot to side, along the line of dance.

Close your right foot to your left foot and swivel slightly to the right to face against the line of dance.

Step right foot to side, against the line of dance (moving to the right, lady to the left).

Cross your left foot over your right foot, against the line of dance.

Step right foot to side, against the line of dance.

Close your left foot to your right foot and swivel slightly to the left to face the line of dance.

Bars 9–12

Release the double hold and take up ballroom hold.

Waltz to the right (1a2, 2a2, 3a2) and open up to end in
starting position on 4a2.
   Bars 13–16

Mississippi Dip

Like the Pride of Erin, this dance originated in Edinburgh. It is essential for every ceilidh, if only for its unusual start and swaying actions, not to mention the plantation type music and songs which give this dance an added fascination.

Time: 4/4
Tempo: 50bpm

Begin in ballroom hold with gent facing the wall and lady facing the centre.

Take three steps back towards the centre (left, right, left).
Close your right foot to your left foot.
Sway to the left along the line of dance by transferring your weight to your left foot.
Sway to the right against the line of dance by transferring your weight back to your right foot.
Take three steps forward towards the wall (left, right, left).
Close your right foot to your left foot.
Sway to the left along the line of dance by transferring your weight to your left foot.

Sway to the right against the line of dance by transferring your weight back to your right foot.
    Bars 1–4

Turn slightly to your left (lady to her right), still in ballroom hold, and walk forward three steps down the line of dance (left, right, left).
Close your right foot to your left foot (lady turns to her left on this step to face against the line of dance).
Take three steps back against the line of dance (right, left, right). Lady takes three steps forward.
Close your right foot to your left foot.
Make two complete natural waltz turns to the right (1a2, 2a2, 3a2, 4a2) to end in side by side position, facing up the line of dance.
    Bars 5–8

Release lady's right hand, keeping your right hand round her waist.
Step left foot forward, down the line of dance.
Step right foot forward and across your left foot with a dipping action – gent bends his right knee, lady bends her left knee.
Step left foot forward, down the line of dance.
Close your right foot to your left foot without weight.
Transfer your weight back to your right foot.
Step left foot forward, down the line of dance.
Step right foot forward and across your left foot with a dipping action.
Step left foot forward, down the line of dance.
Close your right foot to your left foot without weight.
Transfer your weight back to your right foot.
    Bars 9–12

Take up ballroom hold.

Turn slightly to your left (lady turns to her right) and walk forward down the line of dance (left, right, left).

Gent closes his right foot to his left foot while lady turns to her left to face against the line of dance.

Gent takes three steps back, against the line of dance (right, left, right), lady takes three steps forward.

Close your right foot to your left foot.

Make two complete waltz turns to the right (1a2, 2a2, 3a2, 4a2) to end with gent facing the wall and lady facing the centre.

Retain ballroom hold and you are ready to begin the dance again.

Bars 13–16

Pride of Erin Waltz

This dance is in big demand at ceilidh, and although its name makes it sound like an Irish dance, it actually originated in Edinburgh. However, it goes perfectly with some beautiful Irish melodies and makes an ideal sing-along waltz.

   Time: 3/4
   Tempo: 40bpm

Begin in double hold with gent facing the wall and lady facing the centre.

Step left foot to side, along the line of dance (lady steps with her right foot).
Cross your right foot over your left foot.
Chassé to left (step, close, step) and turn, pointing your right foot against the line of dance.
   Bars 1–4

Step right foot to side, against the line of dance (lady steps with her left foot).
Cross your left foot over your right foot.

Chassé to right (step, close, step) and turn, pointing your left foot along the line of dance.

Bars 5–8

Cross your left foot over your right foot and point your right foot to the side.

Cross your right foot over your left foot and point your left foot to the side.

Bars 9–12

Gent releases lady's right hand.

He turns left and she turns right.

Step left foot forward, down the line of dance and start to turn to left.

Step right foot to side, facing the centre, and close your left foot to your right foot. You should now be back to back with your partner.

Step left foot forward, against the line of dance, continuing to turn to the left.

Step right foot to side, facing the wall, and close your left foot to your right foot. You should now be facing the wall and your partner in double hold.

Bars 13–16

Balance towards your partner (step forward on your left foot and close your right foot to your left foot without weight).

Balance away from your partner (step back on your right foot and close your left foot to your right foot without weight).

Gent releases partner's left hand and you waltz to each other's places, passing left hip to left hip, and lady turns under gent's left arm. Gent now faces the centre and lady faces the wall.

Bars 17–20

Pride of Erin Waltz

Balance towards your partner.
Balance away from your partner.
Gent releases partner's left hand and you waltz back to your own place, passing left hip to left hip. Lady again turns under his left arm. End by facing your partner in double hold.
   Bars 21–24

Chassé to the left, along the line of dance (step, close, step).
Chassé back against the line of dance (step, close, step).
   Bars 25–28

Take up ballroom hold and waltz to the right for two complete waltz turns.
   Bars 29–32

The popular party version of this dance has a slight variation in Bars 1–8, as follows:
Both lady and gent are facing the line of dance, the lady on the gent's right side with his right arm round the lady's waist.
Step forward on gent's left foot (lady's right) and swing right foot forward and back.
Take three steps forward and turn on the fourth to face against the line of dance.
   Bars 1–4

Step forward on gent's right foot (lady's left) and swing left foot forward and back.
Take three steps forward against the line of dance and turn on the fourth to face partner and take up double hold.
   Bars 5–8

The remainder of the dance is danced as shown in the first version.

Southern Rose Waltz

This is yet another popular waltz and is especially good as a follow-up to the St Bernard's Waltz.

Time: 3/4
Tempo: 48bpm

Begin in ballroom hold with gent facing the wall and lady facing the centre.
Step to the side on your left foot (lady steps on her right foot).
Close your right foot to your left foot.
Step to the side on your left foot.
Close your right foot to your left foot.
Step to the side on your left foot.
Close your right foot to your left foot, lowering your heels.
　Bars 1–4

Gent now takes lady's right hand in his left and they raise their joined hands.
Step to the side on your left foot (lady steps on her right foot).

Close your right foot to your left foot.
Step to the side on your left foot.
Close your right foot to your left foot.
Step to the side on your left foot.
Close your right foot to your left foot and lower your heel.
During the last four bars lady dances two underarm turns to the right (count 1-2-3, 2-2-3, 3-2-3, 4-2-3).
  Bars 5–8

Take up ballroom hold.
Step to the side on your left foot (lady steps on her right foot).
Close your right foot to your left foot.
Step to the side on your left foot.
Close your right foot to your left foot.
Step to the side on your left foot.
Close your right foot to your left foot (lowering heels).
  Bars 9–12

Waltz turn to the right to end facing the wall (count 1-2-3, 2-2-3, 3-2-3, 4-2-3).
  Bars 13–16

Walk back towards the centre (left, right, left, right). Your partner walks forward.
  Bars 17–20

Walk forward towards the wall (left, right, left, right). Your partner walks backwards.
  Bars 21–24

Still in the ballroom hold, make a slight turn to gent's left (lady's right).

Travel two steps up the line of dance (left, right).
Point your outside foot forward (gent's left, lady's right
foot).
Point the same foot behind (while bending your knees as
in a curtsy).
    Bars 25–28

Waltz turn to the right (count 1-2-3, 2-2-3, 3-2-3, 4-2-3)
and end facing the wall back in your starting position.
    Bars 29–32

Square Tango

This dance is now appearing more frequently in ceilidh, largely because of its simplicity. The Square Tango takes its name from the pattern made by the steps of the first two bars. The dance is described here in its simplest form and makes a perfect introduction to tango.

   Time: 2/4
   Tempo: 32bpm

Begin in ballroom hold with gent facing the line of dance.

Step left foot forward, down the line of dance.
Step your right foot to the side.
Close your left foot to your right foot.
Step right foot back, against the line of dance.
Step your left foot to the side.
Close your right foot to your left foot and so complete the square.

Move your left foot to the side in a longer than usual step.
Slowly close your right foot to your left foot, dragging it without weight.

Move your right foot to the side in a longer than usual step.
Slowly close your left foot to your right foot, dragging it without weight.

   Bars 1–4

Step left foot forward, down the line of dance.
Step your right foot to the side.
Close your left foot to your right foot.
Step right foot back, against the line of dance.
Step your left foot to the side.
Close your right foot to your left foot and so complete the second square.

Move your left foot to the side in a longer than usual step.
Slowly close your right foot to your left foot, dragging it without weight.
Move your right foot to the side in a longer than usual step.
Slowly close your left foot to your right foot, dragging it without weight.

   Bars 5–8

Left foot forward, down the line of dance – slow.
Right foot forward, down the line of dance – slow.
Left foot forward, down the line of dance – quick.
Right foot forward, down the line of dance – quick.
Left foot forward, down the line of dance – slow.
Right foot forward, down the line of dance – slow.
Left foot forward, down the line of dance – quick.
Right foot forward, down the line of dance – quick.
Left foot forward and begin to turn right – slow.
Right foot forward and complete the turn to face the wall – slow.

   Bars 9–12

Step your left foot to the side, still facing the wall.

Transfer your weight back on to your right foot.

Replace your weight on to your left foot (balance) and begin to turn to the right.

Step your right foot forward (taking only a small step) with rocking action and continue the turn to the right.

Step your left foot back (again, only a small step) with rocking action, still turning right.

Step right foot forward (small step) with rocking action, still turning right.

Step left foot back (small step) with rocking action, still turning right.

Transfer your weight back on to your right foot. You should now be facing the line of dance, having completed a full turn to the right.

Bars 13–16

A simple way of learning these bars is to start from the last slow step on bar 12 (which was right foot forward, turning to right to face the wall) and count 1, 2 and dip on 3, then count 4, 5, 6, 7, 8 while making a rocking turn (transferring your weight from one foot to the other) and dip on 9.

You are now ready to start the dance again.

Strip the Willow

This set dance has appealed to all ages for many years. Its lively music makes it popular in schools and at weddings, as well as at ceilidhs.

Time: 64-bar jig

Form a set made up of four couples with ladies facing gents (this is called a longways set).
Gent stands with his left shoulder towards the top of the room (normally, this is where the band are) and lady has her right shoulder towards the top of the room.

The first couple (the couple nearest the stage) link their right arms and swing each other round at the top of the set for a count of 16.
Bars 1–8

The first lady turns the second gent with her left arm and then her partner with her right arm and repeats this down to the last gent at the bottom of the set.
Bars 9–20

The first couple link their right arms and swing each other at the bottom of the set for a count of 16.
   Bars 21–28

The first gent turns the fourth lady with his left arm and then his partner with his right arm and repeats this with each lady in turn until he reaches the top of the set again.
   Bars 29–40

The first couple link their right arms and swing at the top of the set for a count of 16.
   Bars 41–48

The first lady turns the second gent with her left arm while first gent turns the second lady with his left arm and then turns his partner by the right arm.
Repeat with each couple until you reach the bottom of the set.
   Bars 49–60

The first couple link their right arms and swing at the bottom of the set. Meanwhile, the second couple have become the couple at the top and so they link right arms and swing each other. The sequence is repeated until each couple in the set have completed the dance.
   Bars 61–64

Veleta

The Veleta is one of the oldest old-time waltzes and still remains very popular. There are two versions; the party version is described on page 57.

Time: 3/4
Tempo: 42bpm

Begin by standing side-by-side (in open hold), facing the line of dance. Lady's left hand should be in gent's right hand.

Step left foot forward, down the line of dance (lady steps with her right foot).
Step right foot forward, down the line of dance.
Close your left foot to your right foot.
Step right foot forward, down the line of dance.
Step left foot forward, down the line of dance, turning slightly to your right to face your partner (lady turns to her left).
Close your right foot to your left foot while releasing lady's left hand and take her right hand in your left hand.
Step left foot to side, along the line of dance.

Slowly drag your right foot to your left foot.
Step left foot to side, along the line of dance.
Slowly drag your right foot to your left foot and now you should be facing against the line of dance.

   Bars 1–4

Step right foot forward, against the line of dance (lady steps with her left foot).
Step left foot forward, against the line of dance.
Close your right foot to your left foot.
Step left foot forward, against the line of dance, turning slightly to your left to face your partner (lady turns to her right).
Step right foot forward, against the line of dance.
Close your left foot to your right foot while releasing lady's right hand and take her left hand in your right hand.
Step right foot to side, against the line of dance.
Slowly drag your left foot to your right foot.
Step right foot to side, against the line of dance.
Slowly drag your left foot to your right foot and now you should be facing your partner.
Take up ballroom hold.

   Bars 5–8

Dance one complete natural turn to the right to end facing the wall and your partner.
Gent releases lady's left hand.
Step left foot to side, along the line of dance.
Slowly drag your right foot to your left foot.
Step left foot to side, along the line of dance.
Slowly drag your right foot to your left foot.

   Bars 9–12

Take up ballroom hold.
Dance three bars of natural waltz turn to gent's right

(1a2, 2a2, 3a2), opening out on 4a2 to return to starting position.

Bars 13–16

Victory Waltz

The Victory Waltz is a little unusual in that the main feature of its movements is the balance.

Time: 3/4
Tempo: 40bpm

Begin by both partners facing diagonal to the wall in shadow hold. (Gent stands slightly behind the lady and to her left. His left hand holds her left hand at shoulder level, and his right hand holds her right hand over her right shoulder.)
Both lady and gent dance the same steps, on the same foot, for bars 1–24.
Step left foot forward, diagonal to the wall, down the line of dance.
Swing your right foot forward, raising it slightly off the floor.
Pivot on your left foot, turning right to face against the line of dance.
Swing your right foot in front of you, raising it slightly off the floor.
Run back three steps (right, left, right).
   Bars 1–4

Walk three steps forward, against the line of dance (left, right, left).
Close your feet together and turn to the left to face diagonal to the wall.
   Bars 5–8

Step left foot forward, diagonal to the wall, down the line of dance.
Swing your right foot forward, raising it slightly off the floor.
Pivot on your left foot, turning right to face against the line of dance.
Swing your right foot in front of you, raising it slightly off the floor.
Run back three steps (right, left, right).
   Bars 9–12

Walk three steps forward, against the line of dance (left, right, left).
Close your feet together and turn to the left to face diagonal to the wall.
   Bars 13–16

Still in shadow hold:
Step left foot forward, diagonal to the wall.
Swing your right foot forward, raising it slightly off the floor.
Step your right foot back.
Step your left foot to the side.
Step your right foot forward, diagonal to the centre.
Swing your left foot in front of you, raising it slightly off the floor.
Step your left foot back.
Step your right foot to the side.
Step your left foot forward, diagonal to the wall.
   Bars 17–20

Swing your right foot in front of you, raising it slightly off the floor, diagonal to the wall.
Step your right foot back.
Step your left foot to the side.
Step your right foot forward, diagonal to the centre.
Swing your left foot in front of you, raising it slightly off the floor, diagonal to the centre.
Step your left foot back.
Step your right foot to the side.
   Bars 21–24

Step your left foot to the side, along the line of dance, while making a slight turn to the right.
Close your right foot to your left, facing the wall and still in shadow hold.
Step, close, step, down the line of dance (left, right, left).
Lady releases gent's left hand and turns right under his raised arm while he dances step, close, step, against the line of dance.
   Bars 25–28

Take up ballroom hold.
Dance a natural waltz turn to right (1 a2, 2a2, 3a2) and open up to shadow hold on 4a2 ready to recommence dance.
   Bars 29–32

Waltz of the Bells

This waltz is made all the more interesting as all the ladies' turns are performed in a bower hold.

Time: 3/4
Tempo: 48bpm

Begin by standing in open hold, both partners facing the line of dance. Lady's left hand should be in gent's right hand.

Step on to your left foot and point your right foot down the line of dance (lady steps on to her right foot and points her left foot).
Step on to your right foot and point your left foot.
Step on to your left foot and point your right foot.
Step on to your right foot and point your left foot.
  Bars 1–4

Release the hold and dance a solo turn (gent turning to his left, lady to her right). Count 1-2-3, 2-2-3.
Take up double hold and chassé to the side (step, close, step, close), along the line of dance.
  Bars 5–8

Gent releases lady's left hand and takes her right hand in his left (in open hold) facing against the line of dance.
Step on to your right foot and point your left foot (lady steps on to left foot and points her right foot).
Step on to your left foot and point your right foot.
Step on to your right foot and point your left foot.
Step on to your left foot and point your right foot.
   Bars 9–12

Release the hold.
Dance a solo natural turn to the right (lady dances a reverse turn to left). Count 1-2-3, 2-2-3.
Take up double hold and step, close, step, close against the line of dance.
Release hold and take your partner's right hand in your right hand and her left hand in your left hand underneath the right hands.
   Bars 13–16

Dance two side closes up the line of dance, raising joined hands and allowing lady to dance a natural turn to right under raised arms (bower hold).
Retaining hold, both dance two side closes along the line of dance.
   Bars 17–20

Dance two side closes against the line of dance, raising joined hands and allowing lady to dance a reverse turn to left under raised arms (bower hold).
Retaining hold, both dance two side closes against the line of dance.
   Bars 21–24

Release your partner's left hand but keep hold of her right hand.

Balance away from your partner (gent steps back on his left foot and closes his right foot to his left foot without weight).
Balance towards your partner (gent steps forward on his right foot and closes his right foot to his left foot without weight).

Balance away from your partner.
Balance towards your partner.
   Bars 25–28

Take up ballroom hold.
Dance a natural waltz, turning to gent's right (1a2, 2a2, 3a2). Open out on 4a2 to resume starting position.
   Bars 29–32

Tartan Wizardry

Challenging Ceilidh Dances

Anniversary Two-Step	125
Billy Jean Swing	127
Duke of Perth	130
Eightsome Reel	133
Fiona's Polka	137
Killarney Waltz	140
La Va	143
Melody Foxtrot	146
Palais Glide	148
Posties Jig	150
Royal Empress Tango	154
Virginia Reel	157

Anniversary Two-Step

This is a progressive dance which proves very popular at ceilidhs and is an excellent mixer.

   Time: 6/8
   Tempo: 56bpm

All couples form a circle round the room, gent facing the wall and lady facing the centre (no hand hold).

Gent takes three steps (left, right, left) back towards the centre. Lady steps back towards the wall (right, left, right). Close your right foot to your left foot without weight. Take three steps (right, left, right) forward towards the wall. Lady steps forward towards the centre (left, right, left). Close your left foot to your right foot without weight – gent moves towards his partner's left side and takes her left hand in his left hand. In his right hand he takes the right hand of the lady on his right. Now everyone's hands are joined and you have formed one grand circle round the room – with ladies facing the centre and gents facing the wall.
   Bars 1–4

Gent pas de basque to left, along the line of dance (lady to right).

Gent pas de basque to right, against the line of dance (lady left).

Release right hand hold. Retaining left hand hold with own partner both walk half turn curving to left (gent left, right, left) (lady right, left, right).

Gent close right foot to left foot — gent now facing the centre and lady facing the wall.

Gent joins right hand with right hand of lady on right side forming a complete circle.

Gent now facing the centre and lady facing the wall.

    Bars 5–8

Gent pas de basque to the left, against the line of dance (lady to her right).

Gent pas de basque to the right, along the line of dance (lady to her left).

Gent releases partner's left hand but retains the right hand of lady on his right. (This is your new partner.)

Both walk a half turn, curving to the right. Gent: right, left, right. Lady: left, right, left.

Gent closes his left foot to his right foot to finish facing his new partner.

Gent places his right hand round lady's waist, his left hand on her shoulder, and she puts her right hand round his waist, her left hand on his shoulder.

    Bars 9–12

Swing your partner with propelled pivot steps to the right for a count of eight.

Release the hold and you are ready to begin the dance again.

    Bars 13–16

Billy Jean Swing

The Billy-Jean Swing is a polka-type dance and the steps go perfectly with Jimmy Shand's 'Bluebell Polka'.

Time: 4/4
Tempo: 38–40bpm

Begin facing the line of dance in ballroom hold.

Chassé to the left (step, close, step). Gent begins on his left foot, lady on her right.
Chassé to the right (step, close, step). Gent begins on his right foot, lady on her left.

Now for a reverse zig-zag and forward lock:
Step left foot forward, turning to the left.
Step your right foot to the side, along the line of dance.
Step left foot back (diagonal to the wall) with your partner on your right-hand side (right hip to right hip) and turn to the right.
Step your right foot to the side to end facing the line of dance in line with your partner. And so you have completed a zig-zag.

Step left foot forward, down the line of dance.
Cross your right foot behind your left foot (this is called a lock step).
Step left foot forward.
   Bars 1–4

Next is a natural zig-zag and forward lock:
Step your right foot forward, down the line of dance, with your partner on your right-hand side and turn to the right.
Step your left foot to the side, along the line of dance.
Step your right foot backwards (diagonal to the centre) with your partner on your left side and turn to the left.
Step your left foot to the side and end facing the line of dance with your partner on your right side and so complete the zig-zag.

Gent steps right foot forward down the line of dance on lady's right side .
Cross your left foot behind your right foot in a lock step.
Step your right foot forward in check (with weight).
Step back with your left foot, against the line of dance.
Cross your right foot in front of your left foot (this step is called a back lock).
Step back with your left foot, against the line of dance, turning to your right.
Chassé to your right (step, close, step) square to partner (facing your partner).
   Bars 5–8

Release the hold and turn outwards, gent to his left and lady to her right.
Step on to your left foot and cross your right foot over your left foot in check (with weight).
Step back on to your left foot and chassé to your right,

going behind lady (lady chassés to her left, in front of gent).

Cross your left foot over your right foot in check (with weight).

Step back on your right foot and chassé to your left behind lady (lady chassés to her right, in front of gent).

   Bars 9–12

Gent and lady dance outward solo turn (gent turning to the left, lady to the right) with bouncy step action and end facing the wall and your partner.

Take up ballroom hold.

Waltz to gent's right in polka time and end facing the line of dance, ready to recommence.

   Bars 13–16

Duke of Perth

This lively Scottish dance, also known as Broun's Reel or as Clean Pease Strae in some areas, is once again a request dance.

Original tune or any good reel.

Form a set made up of four couples with ladies facing gents (this is called a longways set).
Gent stands with his left shoulder towards the top of the room (normally, this is where the band are) and lady has her right shoulder towards the top of the room.

The first couple (the couple nearest the stage) take each other's right hands and turn each other. Gent passes behind second gent and lady passes behind second lady – the second couple now move into first couple's place at the top of the set. (This is called casting off a place.)
    Bars 1–4

The first couple now meet in the centre of the set and join their left hands for one and a half turns to finish facing the first corner – gent faces the third lady and his partner faces the second gent. In ceilidh, the first corner means the person on your right-hand side.

Bars 5–8

Take the right hands of your 'first corner' and turn. Then turn your own partner with your left hand to finish facing the opposite corner – gent faces second lady and lady faces third man. The opposite corner is, therefore, the person on your left-hand side.

Bars 9–12

Take the right hand of your 'opposite corner' and turn. Then turn your own partner with your left hand to finish facing first corner again.

Bars 13–16

The first couple now set to and turn their first corners with double-hand hold – gent sets to and turns third lady, his partner turns second gent.

Bars 17–20

The first couple now set to and turn their opposite corners with double-hand hold – gent sets to and turns second lady, his partner turns third gent.

Bars 21–24

The first gent dances a reel of three (also called a figure of eight) with his two corner partners (third and second lady) and the first lady dances a reel of three with her two corner partners (second and third gent).

The first couple cross over to their own sides, one place down (the second couple keep their place at the top of the set).

The first couple repeat the whole sequence with the third and fourth couples.

Once completed they should be at the bottom of the set (they are now the fourth couple) and the second couple (now the first couple) are ready to start again.
  Bars 25–32

Quick Reminder

Four couples to a set

First couple turn with right hands and cast off one place. First couple turn each other with left hands for 1½ turns to end facing first corner.

Turn first corner with right hand.
Turn partner with left hand.
Turn second corner with right hand.
Turn partner with left hand to end facing first corner.

Set to and turn the first corners in double-hand hold.
Set to and turn the second corners in double-hand hold.

Reel of three with respective corner partners.
Then first couple cross to own side one place down.

Eightsome Reel

There are various versions of the Eightsome Reel so we would advise you to 'go with the flow' in whichever area you dance.

This is a four couple set dance of 40, 8×48, 40 bar reels, best danced to original tune.

First couple stand with their backs to the band.
Second couple stand on first couple's left-hand side.
Third couple stand facing first couple and the band.
Fourth couple stand on first couple's right-hand side, (making a square formation).

All couples join hands and circle to the left for eight steps.
   Bars 1–4

All couples then circle to the right for eight steps, finishing in starting positions.
   Bars 5–8

Release hands and gent takes partner's left hand in his right hand.

Ladies move to the centre, joining their right hands in a star formation.
All dance round clockwise for four steps.
Bars 9–12

Keep hold of your partner's hand and turn to the right so that gents can join their left hands to form a star.
All dance four steps back to original position.
Bars 13–16

Turn right to face your own partner and set twice to partner (four pas de basque).
Bars 17–20

Turn your partner twice to the right in a double-hand hold for a count of eight.
Bars 21–24

Release the hold and face your partner. You are now going to dance a Grand Chain:
Take your partner's right hand in your right hand and pass right shoulder to right shoulder.
Take the left hand of next lady (lady takes left hand of next gent) in your left hand and pass left shoulder to left shoulder.
Continue in this manner until you reach your own partner again.
(Gents are travelling anti-clockwise and ladies clockwise along the chain.)
Bars 25–40

First lady (nearest the band) dances into the centre of the circle.

First lady dances a solo pas de basque while the other seven dancers join hands and circle to the left for a count of eight.

Bars 1–4

All circle back to the right for eight.

Bars 5–8

Lady in the centre then faces her own partner and dances two pas de basque.

Then she takes her partner in a double hold and turns him.

Bars 9–12

Lady in the centre then turns to face the gent opposite her partner and dances two pas de basque steps and turns him.

Bars 13–16

She then turns to her partner and dances a figure of eight with him and gent opposite, beginning by passing her own partner left shoulder to left shoulder.

Bars 17–24

Lady dances into the centre again and dances pas de basque steps while the other seven dancers circle to the left for a count of eight and back to the right for eight.

Lady in the centre now turns to the fourth gent and repeats the above steps with fourth and second gent. At end of the figure of eight she returns to her own place, beside her partner, and second lady moves into the centre.

The first lady's steps are repeated by the second, third and fourth ladies. Then each gent takes his turn.
Bars 25–48

To complete the dance repeat the first section of the dance (bars 1–40).
Bars 1–40

Fiona's Polka

This dance fits well with 'Fiona's Wedding' or any other polka tune.

Time: 4/4
Tempo: 38–40bpm

Begin by both partners facing the line of dance in shadow hold. (Gent stands slightly behind the lady and to her left. His left hand holds her left hand at shoulder level, and he takes her right hand in his right hand over her right shoulder.)
Both gent and lady dance the same steps (with the same foot) as follows:

Step heel, toe, heel, toe with your left foot.
Step left foot forward, making a slight turn towards the centre.
Cross your right foot behind your left foot (this step is called a lock).
Step left foot forward, making a slight turn to the right.
Step heel, toe, heel, toe with your right foot.
Step right foot forward, making a slight turn towards the wall.

Cross your left foot behind your right foot in a lock step.
Step right foot forward.
   Bars 1–4

Cross your left foot over your right foot towards the wall.
Make a slight turn to your left and point your right foot to the side.
Step right foot forward, moving towards the centre.
Cross your left foot behind your right foot in a lock step.
Step right foot forward, turning slightly to the right.
Point your left foot to the side.
Step left foot forward towards the wall.
Cross your right foot behind your left foot in a lock step.
Step left foot forward towards the wall, making a slight turn to face the line of dance.
Close your right foot to your left foot (lady closes her right foot to her left foot without weight.
   Bars 5–8

Release the hold. Gent polka steps (step, close, step, hop) towards the centre. Lady polka steps towards the wall.
Polka step (step, close, step, hop) towards the wall and your partner (lady polka steps towards the centre). End by facing your partner in double hold.
Step left foot forward, down the line of dance.
Point your right foot forward, down the line of dance.
Step right foot forward, down the line of dance.
Point your left foot forward, down the line of dance.
   Bars 9–12

Take up ballroom hold.
Polka natural turn to right (step, close, step, hop – step, close, step, hop – step, close, step, hop – step, close, step,

close), releasing ballroom hold and opening out to
shadow hold.

    Bars 13–16

Killarney Waltz

This is a waltz with a challenge. You can have lots of fun trying to master the unusual swivel and zig-zag steps.

   Time: 3/4
   Tempo: 48bpm

Begin in open hold, facing the line of dance. Lady's left hand should be in gent's right hand.

Step on to your left foot and point your right foot down the line of dance (lady steps on to her right foot and points her left foot).
Step on to your right foot and point your left foot down the line of dance. Release hold.
Make a solo outward turn to your left (lady turns to her right) and end facing against the line of dance with lady's right hand in gent's left hand (open hold).
   Bars 1–4

Step on to your right foot and point your left foot (lady steps on to her left foot and points her right foot) against the line of dance.

Step on to your left foot and point your right foot. Release hold.

Make a solo outward turn to your right (lady turns to her left) and end facing down the line of dance.

   Bars 5–8

Gent takes his partner's right hand in his left.

Gent dances two side closes down the line of dance while lady goes under their joined raised arms (lady turning 1-2-3, 2-2-3).

Lady dances two side closes down the line of dance while gent goes under their joined arms (gent turning 1-2-3, 2-2-3).

   Bars 9–12

Take up double hold.

Walk, walk, chassé, down the line of dance and turn to face against the line of dance.

Walk, walk, chassé, against the line of dance. On the last step gent turns to face diagonal to the wall.

   Bars 13–20

Step left foot back and swivel one quarter turn to gent's right.

Step right foot back (check).

Step left foot forward, right foot to side and left foot back while making a quarter turn to the left to face diagonal to the wall.

Step right foot forward, diagonal to the wall, and make a quarter turn to the right to face diagonal to the wall, against the line of dance.

Step left foot forward (check).

Step right foot back and left foot to side while making a quarter turn to the left to face diagonal to the wall.

Step right foot forward on the outside of your partner

and take up ballroom hold.
   Bars 21–28

Waltz to the right (1a2, 2a2, 3a2), opening out to starting position on 4a2.
   Bars 29–32

La Va

The La Va is another request dance which has been neglected in modern ceilidh programmes and is worthy of a revival. It should be danced to it's own particular tune, also called 'La Va'.

Begin in ballroom hold with gent facing the wall and lady facing the centre.

Hop on to your right foot.
Step on to your left foot.
Step on to your right foot.
Step on to your left foot and point your right foot to the side while making a half turn to the right to end facing the centre.
(Hop one, two, three, point.)

Hop on your left foot.
Step on to your right foot.
Step on to your left foot.
Step on to your right foot and point your left foot to the side while making a half turn to the right to end facing the wall.
(Hop one, two, three, point.)

Continue dancing and turning in this manner until you have completed eight half turns. Gent should be facing the wall.

Bars 1–16

Moving down the line of dance:
Hop on your right foot.
Step on to your left foot, then on to your right foot.
Hop on your right foot.
Step on to your left foot, then on to your right foot.
(Hop one, two, hop one, two.)

Hop on your right foot.
Step on to your left foot.
Step on to your right foot.
Step on to your left foot and point your right foot to the side while making a half turn to the right to end facing the centre.
(Hop one, two, three, point.)

Still moving down the line of dance:
Hop on your left foot.
Step on to your right foot, then on to your left foot.
Hop on your left foot.
Step on to your right foot, then on to your left foot.
(Hop one, two, hop one, two.)

Hop on your left foot.
Step on to your right foot.
Step on to your left foot.
Step on to your right foot and point your left foot to the side while making a half turn to the right to end facing the wall.
(Hop one, two, three, point.)

Repeat as above till four half-turns have been completed and end facing the wall. Small steps should be taken throughout the dance.
Now you are ready to recommence the dance.
Bars 17–32

Melody Foxtrot

This dance is a simple introduction to foxtrot rhythm. It can be danced to a Harry Lauder type medley, which would add a Scottish flavour to this popular ceilidh dance.

Time: 4/4
Tempo: 32bpm

Begin in ballroom hold.
Step left foot forward, down the line of dance.
Step your right foot to the side.
Close your left foot to your right foot.
Step right foot back, against the line of dance.
Step left foot to the side.
Close your right foot to your left foot (and complete the square).
Walk two steps down the line (left, right), checking on step two.
Transfer your weight back on to your left foot.
Close your right foot to your left foot, then step left foot forward (twinkle).
Cross your right foot behind your left foot (a lock step).
    Bars 1–4

Repeat the square step, as above.

Repeat the twinkle step, as above.

Lock your right foot behind your left foot on the outside of your partner (passing right hip to right hip) and take up double hold.

   Bars 5–8

Step and check your right foot outside your partner (positioning yourselves right side by side).

Replace your weight on to your left foot, turning right.

Step your right foot to the side, against the line of dance.

Step left foot forward, outside your partner (left hip to left hip).

Step and check your left foot, outside your partner (left hip to left hip).

Replace your weight on to your right foot, turning left.

Step your left foot to the side, down the line of dance.

Step your right foot forward and now you should be facing the line of dance with partner square and still in double hold.

   Bars 9–12

Step and check your right foot forward, down the line of dance.

Take up ballroom hold.

Run back three steps (left, right, left).

Close your right foot to your left foot.

Walk two steps down the line of dance (left, right).

Step left foot forward, down the line of dance.

Close your right foot to your left foot.

Side close to the centre (step your left foot to the side and close your right foot to your left foot).

   Bars 13–16

Palais Glide

This is a steady, easy-going dance which is suitable for all ages. The Palais Glide has seen some changes to its steps in recent years but the original version retains its popularity. Here we have described it as a couple's dance but it can also be danced in lines of four or more.

  Time: 4/4
  Tempo: 32bpm

Begin by both partners facing the line of dance in shadow hold. (Gent stands slightly behind the lady and to her left. His left hand holds her left hand at shoulder level, and he takes her right hand in his right hand over her right shoulder.)
Both gent and lady dance the same steps (with the same foot) as follows:

Palais Glide step to right:

Tap your left heel forward without weight (slow).
Step back on your left foot (quick).
Step to the side with your right foot (quick).

Palais Glide

Step your left foot forward (slow).

Palais Glide step to left:

Tap your right heel forward without weight (slow).
Step back on your right foot (quick).
Step to the side with your left foot (quick).
Step your right foot forward (slow).

Palais Glide step to right:

Tap your left heel forward without weight (slow).
Step back on your left foot (quick).
Step to the side with your right foot (quick).
Step your left foot forward (slow).

Cross your right foot behind your left foot – this is called a lock step – (quick).
Step forward on your left foot (small step) (quick).
Step forward on your right foot (slow).
Point your left foot to the side, down the line of dance, while making a quarter turn to the right (slow).
Cross your left foot over your right foot. (slow).
Point your right foot to the side, against the line of dance, while making a quarter turn to the left to face the line of dance (slow).
Run three steps forward (right, left, right), down the line of dance (quick, quick, slow).

Now you are ready to start again.

Posties Jig

This Scottish country dance has found its way into many ceilidhs and is well worth including in any ceilidh programme.

Any good Scottish jig tune (32 bar)

Form a set made up of four couples with ladies facing gents (this is called a longways set).
Gent stands with his left shoulder towards the top of the room (normally, this is where the band are) and lady has her right shoulder towards the top of the room. The couples are numbered from one to four, starting with couple number one who are nearest the band.

First and fourth couples set and cast off one place. Taking their partner's right hands the couples turn each other. First gent turns left, passing behind other gents, and first lady turns right, passing behind other ladies, while fourth gent turns right and fourth lady turns left – and they change places with the second and third couples who now move into first and fourth couple position.
   Bars 1–4

First couple dance half a figure of eight round the second couple.

At the same time, the fourth couple dance half a figure of eight round the third couple.

Bars 5–8

First and fourth gents join their inside hands and make an arch crossing over whilst first and fourth ladies join inside hands and cross over, passing under the gents' raised hands.

The couples crossing over give their free hands to their corners (the person on your right and left-hand side) and turn them, leaving the corners back in their own places.

Bars 9–12

First and fourth couples now join hands with their own partners — the first couple should have their backs towards the band and the fourth standing opposite.

The fourth couple join their inside hands and make an arch, crossing over whilst first couple cross over passing under the arch.

Couples crossing over give their free hands to their corners and turn them, leaving the corners back in their own places.

Bars 13–16

First and fourth gents join their inside hands and make an arch crossing over whilst first and fourth ladies join inside hands and cross over passing under the arch.

Couples crossing over give their free hands to their corners and turn them, leaving the corners back in their own places.

Bars 17–20

First and fourth couples now join their inside hands with their own partners, with the first couple now facing towards the band and the fourth couple opposite.

First couple form an arch and cross over whilst the fourth couple cross over and under the arch. Couples crossing over give their free hands to corners and turn them leaving the corners back in their own places.

First and fourth couple have now turned the four corners.

Bars 21–24

First couple are now in position two (on wrong side of dance).

Fourth couple are now in position three (on wrong side of dance).

First and fourth couple dance half rights and lefts and end up with first couple in third position and fourth couple in second position.

Bars 25–28

First and fourth couple join right hands and make one full turn.

Bars 29–32

Helpful Hints

Set to partner – pas de basque left and right.

Cast-off – in this instance first gent turns left and first lady turns right, while fourth gent turns right and fourth lady turns left at the same time.

Half a figure eight – dance half a figure eight crossing over and dancing round one partner.

Half right and half left – turn your partner with your right hand and then turn person on your right with your left hand.

Quick Reminder

First and fourth couple set and cast off one place.
The first couple dance half a figure eight round the second couple.
The fourth couple dance half a figure eight round the third couple.

First and fourth gents make an arch and cross over.
First and fourth ladies pass under, giving free hands to corners and turn.
Finish when corners are in their own place.
First couple should be facing down and fourth couple facing up.

Repeat up and down, fourth couple making arch.
Repeat back to places.
First and fourth couple dance half rights and lefts.
First and fourth couple turn with right hands back to own side.
First couple are now in second place and fourth couple in third place.

Royal Empress Tango

This traditional tango has stood the test of time and still retains its popularity.

Time: 2/4
Tempo: 32bpm

Begin in ballroom hold, facing the line of dance.

Step left foot forward, down the line of dance.
Step right foot forward, down the line of dance, slightly flexing your right knee.
Step left foot back, against the line of dance.
Step right foot back, against the line of dance.
The following steps are performed while moving diagonal to the centre:
Chassé to the left (step forward on your left foot, close your right foot to your left foot, step forward on your left foot).
The following steps are performed while moving diagonal to the wall:
Chassé to the right (step forward on your right foot, close your left foot to your right foot, step forward on your right foot).

Turn to your left on the last step and prepare to move to the centre in side-by-side position (gent's right hip against lady's left hip).

    Bars 1–4

Take two steps forward towards the centre (left, right).
Step left foot forward, towards the centre.
Close your right foot to your left foot.
Step left foot forward, towards the centre, and swivel to your right to end facing the wall, leaving your right foot extended. (Gent's left hip against lady's right hip.)
Take two steps forward towards the wall (right, left).
Right foot forward, towards the wall.
Close your left foot to your right foot.
Step right foot forward, towards the wall, gent turning his partner to her right.
Almost close your left foot to your right foot without weight (gent's right hip against lady's left hip). Now you both should be facing down the line of dance.

    Bars 5–8

Now for a pivot turn:
Step left foot forward, down the line of dance.
Step right foot forward, down the line of dance, beginning to turn right.
Step left foot back, down the line of dance, pivoting strongly to the right to end facing the line of dance (lady steps forward on her right foot, between her partner's feet, while pivoting strongly to right to end facing the line of dance).
Step right foot forward, down the line of dance
Almost close your left foot to your right foot without weight and point your left foot.

Take two steps forward in promenade position, down the

line of dance (left, right).

Point your left foot forward, down the line of dance, and swivel to your right on the balls of your feet (lady swivels to the left), finishing with weight on left foot. Leave your right foot extended and now you should be facing against the line of dance.

Bars 9–12

Step right foot forward, against the line of dance.

Step left foot forward, against the line of dance.

Point your right foot forward, against the line of dance and swivel to the left on the balls of your feet (lady swivelling to right), finishing with weight on right foot. Leave your left foot extended.

Turn slightly to the right, square to your partner.

Dance a rotary natural chassé turn to the right as follows:

Step your left foot to the side, beginning to turn right.

Close your right foot to your left foot, still turning right.

Step your left foot back, down the line of dance.

Step your right foot to the side, still turning right.

Close your left foot to your right foot, still turning right.

Step right foot forward, down the line of dance.

Now you should be facing down the line of dance and be ready to recommence the dance.

Bars 13–16

Virginia Reel

This is the most popular of the American square dances. A toe-tapping, hip-swinging dance, the Virginia Reel will have everyone up on the floor and raring to go.

Time: 6/8
Tempo: 48bpm

Form a set made up of four couples with ladies facing gents (this is called a longways set).
Gent's left shoulder and lady's right shoulder are towards the top of the room (where the band is).

Ladies join hands and gents join hands.
All advance towards each other.
All retire.
Bars 1–4

All advance towards each other.
All retire.
Bars 5–8

Walk towards your partner, grasp right hands and turn.

Retire to original place.
  Bars 9–12

Walk towards your partner, grasp left hands and turn.
Retire to original place.
  Bars 13–16

Walk towards partner, grasp both hands and turn.
Retire to original place.
  Bars 17–20

Do-si-do round your partner (pass right shoulder to right
shoulder). Step to your right – you should now be back
to back – and then pass left shoulder to left shoulder and
return to your original place. Turn to face your partner on
the last step.
  Bars 21–24

First gent links his partner's right arm with his and swings
down the centre of the lines to the bottom of the set.
  Bars 25–32

First couple release their hold and gent links his left arm
with that of the fourth lady. At the same time, lady links
her left arm with that of the fourth gent and both couples
make two complete turns.
First couple link their right arms and turn.
Continue this routine until you reach the top of the set.
  Bars 33–48

When first couple come to the top of the set they cast
off, gents turning left and following the first gent down
the outside of the set and ladies turning right following
the first lady.
When they meet at the bottom of the set, the partners

join hands and follow the first couple to the top of the set.
Bars 49–56

As first couple reach top of set they turn and change hands (gent takes lady's right hand in his left) and form an arch.
First couple now move down the set while other couples move up under this arch.
First couple should now be in fourth place and the second couple have become the first couple ready to start the dance again.
Bars 57–64

There are many variations of this dance.